CW00468638

Engendering Emotions

Engendering Emotions

Alan Petersen

School of Sociology, Politics and Law
University of Plymouth, UK

First published 2004 by
PALGRAVE MACMILLAN
Houndmills, Basingstoke, Hampshire RG21 6XS and
175 Fifth Avenue, New York, N.Y. 10010
Companies and representatives throughout the world

PALGRAVE MACMILLAN is the global academic imprint of the Palgrave
Macmillan division of St. Martin's Press, LLC and of Palgrave Macmillan Ltd.
Macmillan® is a registered trademark in the United States, United Kingdom
and other countries. Palgrave is a registered trademark in the European
Union and other countries.

ISBN 0–333–99737–9 hardback

This book is printed on paper suitable for recycling and made from fully
managed and sustained forest sources.

A catalogue record for this book is available from the British Library.

Library of Congress Cataloging-in-Publication Data
Petersen, Alan R., Ph. D.
    Engendering emotions / Alan Petersen.
        p.   cm.
    Includes bibliographical references and index.
    ISBN 0–333–99737–9
    1. Emotions—Sex differences.   2. Sex differences (Psychology)   I. Title.

BF531.P48 2004
155.3′3—dc22

                                                                        2004048581

10   9   8   7   6   5   4   3   2   1
13   12   11   10   09   08   07   06   05   04

Printed and bound in Great Britain by
Antony Rowe Ltd, Chippenham and Eastbourne

To Ros Porter

Contents

Acknowledgements

I wish to thank all those who have assisted me during the preparation of this book, including Jennifer Nelson, Briar Towers, and Heather Gibson at Palgrave Macmillan. I am grateful to Sam Regan deBere, Matthew David, David Mason, Sylvia Waldby, and Rachel Woodward who offered items of information or source material. I am especially indebted to Iain Wilkinson for his stimulating conversations and suggestions for reading. Sue Tagg has helped in numerous ways, and I am grateful to her. Some of the material appearing in Chapter 2 first appeared in *Journal of Gender Studies* (Vol. 6, No. 3, 1997). I thank Deirdre Davies for collecting and helping to analyse the data that provided the basis for that article, and Taylor & Francis (http://www.tandf.co.uk) for granting me permission to reproduce the material here. I doubt that this book would have been possible without the love and support of Ros Porter.

1
Conceptualising Gender and Emotion

The question of what distinguishes men and women emotionally and intellectually has been an abiding interest of scholars, journalists, popular writers, and lay people alike in the contemporary West. Although debate about such differences can be traced back to antiquity, this interest has become especially pronounced over the last two hundred years. Natural scientists, social scientists, philosophers, and feminists have all contributed to thinking about gender-based emotional differences, asking such questions as, to what extent and exactly how do men and women differ emotionally? What defines and how can one best account for apparent differences? Should differences be celebrated or denigrated? And, insofar as there are differences, what does this mean for how people live their lives and conduct their relationships? Scholars have developed a diverse body of theory and empirical work on the topic of gender-based emotional difference and, by this means, have shaped wider public discourse about men, women, and emotionality. It is in popular media, such as self-help guides, magazines, news media, and movies, however, that the preoccupation with difference is perhaps most evident. Such media would seem to be a major source for public knowledge about gender and emotion and a significant means for disseminating views on difference. Books such as Moir and Moir's *Why Men Don't Iron* (1998), Gray's *Men Are From Mars, Women Are From Venus* (1992), and Pease and Pease's *Why Men Don't Listen and Women Can't Read Maps* (2001) have enjoyed a wide readership and generated much debate. This suggests a ready market for the consumption of their messages. These forms of media offer insights into current anxieties about gender-based emotional differences, as well as providing 'windows' for examining changing constructions of femininity and masculinity.

Drawing on a diverse range of sources, this book examines the production and promotion of the idea of difference in male and female emotionality in the contemporary West. In focusing on the contemporary West, I am not suggesting that a concern with such difference has been absent in earlier periods and in non-Western societies. Indeed, I contend that many contemporary Western ideas about sex or gender difference in temperament or emotion can be traced back to an earlier period and today increasingly circulate in non-Western societies. However, as I argue, contemporary Western societies have distinctive features of social organisation and culture that make difference, particularly emotional difference, especially salient. Prevailing systems of knowledge and modes of regulation in the public sphere (at work and in the broader society) and in the private sphere (at home, and with intimates and family members) highlight and reinforce difference, shaping conceptions of self and social relations. The valuing of science and expertise is a central characteristic of contemporary culture, profoundly shaping how people see the world and respond to and interact with others. Rational science is the source of many ideas about difference, including emotional difference, and has legitimated policies that are based on assumptions of difference. Science and expertise reflect dominant social priorities and serve to buttress particular interests and political programmes. This book aims to highlight how scientific theories of emotion have served, and serve, in the fabrication and regulation of difference and the reproduction of particular social arrangements. In so doing, it seeks to encourage reflection on the potential for alternative constructions of gender and emotion and for the development of supportive policies and practices and on how one might, at the level of the individual, resist the expectations associated with ascribed gender roles. In this chapter, I outline my assumptions and guiding concepts, and begin to develop the argument, and then finish with a summary of the content of the chapters that follow.

The concept of engendered emotions

The basic guiding premise of this book is that 'emotions', far from signifying fixed attributes of the person, are *engendered*. 'Emotions' are *engendered* in two senses. First, 'emotions' are an achievement or production, and hence are subject to change. The idea that emotions are produced or 'constructed' is widespread in contemporary social science. However, the idea has come to prominence only relatively recently and is by no means uncontested. Ideas about emotions mirror changing views about the status of knowledge and truth, and about the relative weight to be ascribed to the universal and the particular, the objective and the subjective, and the natural and the cultural in explanation. Psychologists have long sought to identify universal emotional states – or unvarying aspects of the person – employing surveys and surrogate measures such as facial expressions to capture and categorise their essential features. The psychology of emotions has changed over time, and generated increasingly complex models, with a growing acknowledgement of the importance of the social context and of learning. However, psychological research has continued to focus largely on biology and on individual cognition (Reddy, 2001: Chapter 1), as though emotions have a stable, definable 'essence'. This denies that there is nothing fixed, 'essential', and universal about emotional experiences or responses. Both the classifications of 'emotion' – the ways of typifying and ordering psychological states and corresponding physiological or behavioural responses – and descriptions or reports of 'emotional' experience may vary considerably *across* cultures and in different contexts *within* cultures. Anthropologists have documented the cross-cultural variability of categories of emotion and emotional experience, and have shown that, outside the West, emotions have been generally regarded as an outcome of social interactions and as not clearly distinguishable from thinking (see, e.g. Fischer and Manstead, 2000; Reddy, 2001: Chapter 2; Wierzbicka, 1999). Although few anthropological studies have focused specifically on gender differences in emotionality across cultures, the notion that emotions are culturally constructed undermines the Western common-sense notion that emotions are biologically based and are feminine (Reddy, 2001: 54). Despite such work, psychological perspectives on emotion prevail and have been highly influential in public discourse on gender and emotion. One of the aims of this book is to reveal how the psychology of emotion reflects and reproduces social views on gender and emotion.

Sociologists can take much of the credit for the idea that emotional experiences and the categories of emotion are 'socially constructed'.

The sociological literature is highly diverse, but includes studies of the role of emotion categories in social interaction, the phenomenology of emotion, the political significance of emotions, and the creation of gendered meanings in emotional experience and expression (e.g. Barbalet, 1998, 2002; Bendelow, 2000; Bendelow and Williams, 1998; Crawford *et al.*, 1992; Denzin, 1984). Durkheim has been described as the 'architect' of the social constructionist approach to emotions, but he also accorded a role to biologically constituted emotions in his theory of social solidarity (Fisher and Chon, 1989). An important, later contributor to the social constructionist approach to emotions has been Norbert Elias, in his historical analysis, *The Civilizing Process: The History of Manners* (1978). Elias saw the rise of bourgeois society as giving rise to an 'emotional economy' demanding and producing a greater self-restraint than was called for in previous, absolutist court societies. He would seem to be one of the first sociologists to make explicit the connections between the norms of emotional expression and the production of particular kinds of selves in modern societies (Elias, 1978: 184–191). Other sociologists since have explored such questions as the construction of the 'emotional self', the impact of dualistic thought on the category of emotion, and how emotional experiences are shaped by social and political contexts. Reflecting sociology's turn away from structural determination in explanation towards acknowledgement of process and agency, recent work has underlined the 'enactment' or 'performance' of emotion. Building on the seminal contribution of Hochschild (1983), *The Managed Heart: The Commercialization of Human Feeling*, scholars have explored aspects of the commodification of emotion and the 'work' involved in presenting the emotional self as well as the physical stresses that may result from the constant monitoring of one's own and others' performances (e.g. Duncombe and Marsden, 1993, 1996, 1998, 2002; Freund, 1998; James, 1989; Wouters, 1991, 1998). These ideas have been highly influential in the developing sub-field of the sociology of emotions as well as in feminism.

The notions of 'emotional work', 'emotional labour', or 'emotional management', employed particularly by feminist scholars, draw attention to the planning, organisation, and physical and psychic expenditure involved in 'performing' emotions in areas of paid and unpaid caring work undertaken predominantly by women. (As I indicate in Chapter 5, the concept of 'emotional management' has, however, found favour among a broader constituency, which has a somewhat different agenda.) Scholars have adopted the above terms in the effort to strategically counter the association of emotionality with irrationality, which in Western society is seen as strongly linked to disorganisation, femininity, and the private sphere of unpaid work. As James comments, to the extent that emotions are thought of as irrational it is difficult to associate them with organisation; however, 'managing them requires anticipation, planning, timetabling and trouble-shooting as does other "work", paid and unpaid' (1989: 27). Just as physical labour can be exploited and commodified through the regulations of the market to create a surplus, it is argued, so emotional labour can be exploited to extract a profit in public and private domains. Since it is women who perform most of the emotional labour, particularly in the private domain of the home, it is they who are predominantly subject to exploitation. In Hochschild's classic study of women flight attendants, the requirement to present a pleasant demeanour to customers necessitated an emotional distancing or alienation by the women, similar to the alienation of the worker from his or her physical labours in the factory (Hochschild, 1983). This brings us to a consideration of the second sense in which emotions are engendered, namely, they are ascribed meanings that tend to be gender-specific.

'Emotion' is not just a descriptive term, signifying a domain of psychological experience or psycho-physiological response. The word evokes particular images, and has associated *evaluative* connotations, that very often attach either to men or to women. Thus, *acting* 'emotionally', 'lovingly', 'passively', 'sensitively', and so on, is strongly associated with *being* 'feminine' while *acting* 'rationally', 'distantly', 'assertively', 'insensitively', and so on tends to be associated with *being* 'masculine'. Such connotations carry imperatives to act, or to interact with others in particular ways. 'Being emotional' is not only strongly associated with 'being feminine' but, as some recent empirical research has revealed, also tends to be seen by both men and women as a weakness and as being in need of control (e.g. Lutz, 1996a,b). As Lutz discovered in her interview-based study with American working- and middle-class women and men, a theme of 'rhetoric of control' was strongly evident in respondents' accounts of emotion. That is, when people are asked to talk about emotions 'one of the most common sets of metaphors used is that in which someone or something controls, handles, copes, deals, disciplines, or manages either or both their emotions or the situation seen as creating the emotion'. That is, 'people typically talk about *controlling* emotions, *handling* emotional situations as well as emotional feelings, and *dealing* with people, situations and emotions' (1996b: 153). As Lutz argues, the notion of control used in discussing the emotions is used in a similar way to its use in discourses on sexuality.

> Both emotionality and sexuality are domains whose understanding is dominated by a biomedical model; both are seen as universal, natural impulses; both are talked about as existing in 'healthy' and 'unhealthy' forms' and both have come under the control of the medical or quasi-medical profession (principally psychiatry and psychology). . . . In addition, the metaphor of control implies something that would otherwise be out of control, something wild and unruly, a threat to order. To speak about controlling emotions is to replicate the view of emotions as natural, dangerous, irrational, and physical. (Lutz, 1996b: 154)

The rhetoric of emotional control reinforces the cultural view of emotion (and implicitly of women as the more emotional gender) as weak, dangerous and irrational, and elevates the social status of those who claim the need or ability to control their own emotions (Lutz, 1996b: 154). Significantly, boys and men who cry are often described as 'sissies', because they are behaving in a girl-like way, that is, weak. A dictionary definition of a sissy is 'an effeminate man or boy', or a 'timid or cowardly person' (Editorial Staff, 1981). It is significant that in Western cultures effeminate men are seen as sexually non-normative (i.e. homosexual) and thus subject to denigration, and timid and gentle men are often seen as weak and therefore in need of 'toughening up' and, in some cases (e.g. the military) punishment. These emotional-gender associations inform popular discourse, scholarly research, and policies in many areas of contemporary social life.

In recent years, a growing number of social scientists have explored the historical and social production of gender-specific emotional norms and conduct. A study by Stearns (1993) examined the recommended standards of emotional expression for men and women in popular advice literature in the nineteenth and early twentieth centuries, showing how these standards served to sustain a growing gap in

gender roles. Crawford *et al.* (1992) employed the method of memory work in their exploration of gender differences in the development of emotions, which they found valuable in their effort to
overcome some of the problems inherent in conventional psychological approaches. Chodorow (1999) adopted a psychoanalytic perspective to examine the dynamics of how people create personal and
emotional meaning and a gender identity throughout their life.
Much of this social science work does challenge the biological, cognitive, and static view of the emotions offered by much psychology
and psychiatry. However, a great deal of scholarly and popular writing takes as 'established fact', and as a point of departure in discussion, that there exist fundamental differences between men and
women in their emotional make-up and experience. Consequently,
the social and political implications of connections between gender
and emotion often remain unexamined.

The political significance of emotions

As William Reddy argues, in his book, *The Navigation of Feeling: A Framework for the History of Emotions* (2001), emotions are both central to
the life of individuals and are subject to profound social influence,
and hence are of 'the highest political significance' (2001: 124). For
a political regime to endure, it must establish a normative order for
the expression of emotions – what he calls an 'emotional regime'.
In Reddy's view, emotional regimes vary according to the strategies
of emotional management, the degree of emotional liberty, the forms
of self-control and the penalties incurred for norm violation. Some
regimes are strict, in that they prescribe how and when individuals
should express emotions and severely penalise 'emotional deviants'.
Other regimes offer such strict emotional discipline in only some
institutions, such as in schools or the military or only at certain times
of the year or at certain stages of life. Such regimes may offer few
constraints on emotional expression, offer a variety of 'emotional
management styles' and allow individuals scope for self-exploration
and relatively unimpeded 'emotional navigation' (2001: 125–126).

   According to Reddy, strict emotional regimes achieve their stability
by offering a restricted vision of human nature and human possibilities.
Because they reduce the scope for 'choice' they produce a higher
incidence of emotional suffering than loose regimes. While this may
be of little importance in the short term, when institutions cope with

events such as war, epidemic, famine, and scarcity, 'in the very long run, they are of the greatest importance'. He notes that emotional regimes become especially salient during times of conquest, colonisation, and expansion, when a normative management strategy is imposed on subject populations. While capitalist democracies would seem to offer great scope for 'emotional navigation', options are limited by contractual relationships (i.e. access to money and property). Reddy notes the large variety of emotional styles in capitalist societies, with class, gender, and ethnic variation being exploited to sustain a complex and inequitable division of labour (2001: 125–128).

The strength of Reddy's analysis, which is an advance on earlier versions of constructionism, is the acknowledgement of links between 'macro' political structures and 'micro' processes of self-formation. That is, he recognises the ways in which broader political regimes may shape and limit emotional expression and self-definition or 'identity'. Thus, one can acknowledge the agency or 'work on the self' involved in emotional labour, without falling into voluntarism (the assumption that actors voluntarily manipulate emotion) and ignoring the political implications of emotional expression, which has been a criticism levelled at constructionist approaches (see, e.g. Barbalet, 1998: 23). With some modification, I believe, Reddy's ideas can be usefully applied to the analysis of gender-emotion associations. Some modification is needed since Reddy's main theoretical concern is with 'emotional liberty' and with demonstrating this concept's value in 'giv[ing] political meaning back to history' (2001: 315), particularly in relation to society's transition to modernity, rather than with the power relations of gender or the formation of gender differences. Reddy has relatively little to say about gender, other than mentioning in passing that it is one of the divisions subject to exploitation by emotional regimes (2001: 128). Nor does he have much to say about the possibilities for contesting constructions of gender and emotion and for nurturing new forms of emotional experience for men and women. In considering these issues, one needs to turn to the work of feminist and masculinity scholars.

The politics of gender-emotion associations

Scholars of gender have long recognised the broad political implications of gender-specific emotion associations. The linking of emotionality with 'femininity' and rationality with 'masculinity' is seen to buttress 'patriarchy' and a gender division of labour that greatly disadvantages women and limits the experiences of men. However, as I pointed out previously (Petersen, 1998, 2004), feminism and the field of men and masculinity studies have suffered from a number of theoretical limitations. Work has failed to escape the very rationalist, hierarchical, and 'essentialist' thinking that has often been the target of criticism. Scholars have found it difficult to move beyond the assumption that men and women have inherent gender-specific capacities or world-views, whether these be style of relating, systems of morality, ethics of care, or temperaments (Petersen, 1998: Chapter 4; 2004: 56–61). The influence of 'gender essentialism' – the premise that there is a fixed, coherent category of gender identity that exists cross-culturally, and can be used as the basis for mobilising those who are seen to share that identity – has limited theoretical development and possibilities for political action. Recent work in the social sciences has critiqued essentialist notions of identity – gender, sexuality, 'race', and so on – and shown them to be based on a pervasive dualistic and hierarchical thinking that has served, and serves, to privilege certain groups while excluding women and sexual and minority ethnic groups. With an increased awareness of the politics of 'identity', scholars recently have begun to emphasise the 'social construction' or 'fabrication' of identity. Consequently, in studies of gender and emotion as in other areas of gender analysis, attention has begun to shift away from viewing gender as a fixed category to a consideration of how gender is *accomplished*. This is reflected in the description of gender as an ongoing 'enactment', 'practice' or 'performance' (Shields, 2000: 6). As West and Zimmerman (1991) express it, we do not *have* a gender, we *do* gender.

Butler (1990), whose work has been especially influential in recent gender debates, uses the notion of performativity to describe the process by which gender is realised. Gender is performative in the sense that it involves the reiteration of known norms or conventions. One needs to be careful to avoid viewing the enactment of gender as simply a matter of individual volition, since our physical bodies (our 'sex') signify a difference that affects how others respond to us and how we act. As Butler (1993) points out, 'sex' – the supposed biological bedrock for the socially constructed 'gender' – is also constructed and rendered intelligible through 'gender'. What we take to be 'sex' is a product of the continual performance of gender.

The notion that there are two genders, male and female, founded on two biological sexes is a historically and culturally specific production. As historical and cross-cultural scholarship has revealed, there are different ways of 'doing' or 'enacting' gender, and different ways of 'making sex' (e.g. Herdt, 1994; Laqueur, 1990; Oyewùmí, 1997). Further, within any given society, factors such as class, ethnicity, nationality, and sexuality influence how gender is lived and experienced (Jackson and Scott, 2002: 21). There is, then, a great deal of ambiguity, fluidity, and indeterminacy about the enactment of gender; its realisation is always incomplete and dependent upon context. Acknowledgement of this permits consideration of how and in what contexts one might challenge conventional ways of 'doing' gender.

In psychology, scholars of gender and emotion have recently begun to embrace the notion of gender as a practice, performance, or accomplishment, and to recognise the importance of social context and learning in the shaping of gender-based emotional experience and expression. Some recent work has sought to offer a corrective to earlier research which is seen to reinforce sexism. The significance of interpersonal relationships and of gender stereotyping, for example in studies involving self-reports, have been increasingly acknowledged in studies on the formation of the gendered self (Shields, 2000: 8–18). However, as Shields observes, the psychology of emotions has yet to move beyond a difference approach to questions of gender and emotion. Focusing on gender difference in itself does not explain how that difference is produced or what maintains it (Shields, 2000: 18). Further, dualistic thinking is evident in the implicit sex/gender model and the assumption of separate and separable biological and socio-cultural realms. Little attention has been paid to the political context shaping psychological research on sex or gender differences, including research undertaken by feminist scholars in the 1970s in their efforts to counter studies of difference that were seen to stereotype women (Eagly, 1995: 149–150). As Eagly argues, although such feminist research has been well intentioned, aiming to dispel people's stereotypes about women by showing differences to be non-existent or by demonstrating that research purporting to show differences is faulty, work has produced findings that conform to people's ideas about 'the sexes' (1995: 153–154).

As in many other areas of gender studies, studies of gender and emotion have failed to interrogate the historical, political, and global processes that shape research agenda, social policies, and public discourse concerning difference. There has been a lack of reflection on the theories of knowledge for studying gender, and lack of recognition of how what counts as knowledge is inevitably shaped by the relationship between 'the knower' and 'the known'. The question of difference – how it is understood, theorised, and acted upon – is a political issue and hence subject to ongoing debate and contestation. In the remainder of this chapter and the chapters that follow, I develop a perspective on gender and emotions that pays attention to issues of context (both global and local), history, and politics, but is 'grounded' in the everyday environments in which men and women live their lives. In the process, I hope both to draw attention to the reductionism of much research in this area to date and to generate novel questions and encourage new lines of enquiry. To begin, since this book focuses centrally on questions of difference, a few words about the concept of difference, as it applies to sex/gender and emotion, are in order.

'Difference'

The notion of 'sex difference' or 'gender difference' (the terms are sometimes used interchangeably and confusingly in the literature) in emotionality or empathy has long been the subject of explicit theorisation, research, and speculation within feminism. For example, in the influential psychoanalytic contribution of Chodorow (1978) ('mothering theory') and the gender justice account of Gilligan (1982) the difference between men and women – in concern for 'the other' and in 'sense of justice' – can be explained by early relationships that result in the formation of different selves (see Chapter 2). This work has been highly influential, supporting the widely held view that there are significant differences between men and women, in ways of relating to others and in notions of justice, although differences are seen largely as socialised rather than biological differences. As mentioned, feminist psychologists have contributed significantly to this literature as part of their efforts to counter stereotypical views about women, but have often inadvertently confirmed people's ideas about 'the sexes'. With the rise and increasing prominence of the genetic worldview (see Miringoff, 1991), some gender theorists have embraced a new perspective on difference. What makes men and women different – psychologically, emotionally and behaviourally – can be accounted for in terms of their genetic make-up (see, e.g. Badinter, 1995; Christen, 1991). The attraction of this for theorists of gender difference is that they do not need to rely on 'soft', difficult-to-measure, socio-cultural data to explain difference. There is seen to be an irreducible, supposedly objective, biological difference between the 'sexes' that can account for apparently obdurate differences in worldviews, behaviours, and emotional responses and experiences. In this account, the 'nature versus nurture' controversy, which has dominated debates in psychology, sociology, and other social sciences during much of the second half of the twentieth century, is seen as misguided. Rather than being the outcome of interaction between biology and culture throughout the lifespan, difference is 'hard-wired' at the outset, with the extent and nature of the difference being influenced to some degree by 'society'.

The 'nature versus nurture' (or 'biology versus society') debate dominates many, if not most, discussions about sex/gender difference. However, it is important to recognise how the level of support for different arguments has varied in response to changing socio-political conditions (see Chapter 5). In the early post-Second World War period, when 'socialisation' theories were favoured, sociologists and social psychologists developed accounts of the acquisition of 'gender identity', often linking these with prescriptions for affirmative social action. The concepts of 'gender' and 'gender identity', originally developed in the social sciences in the 1950s and 1960s in the context of the case management of children of ambiguous sex (Hausman, 1995: 102–108), offered feminists new tools for challenging the notion of biology-as-destiny. The idea of a 'socially constructed' difference runs counter to the idea that women are 'naturally' inclined to nurture and to undertake domestic labour and that men are inherently competitive and adapted to the world of paid work. It implies the need for social interventions to redress inequalities such as better schooling, equal opportunity, equal pay, and better childcare. Many policies focusing on these areas emerged during the period of welfare expansion. However, from the mid-1970s, with the emergence of a more economically liberalised and de-regulated context, and a growing emphasis on private provision, user-pays, self-care, self-reliance, and so on, there has been less support among politicians and various authorities for these policies. This is not to say that socially progressive policies have completely disappeared; however, in the context of advanced liberalism, the value of such policies has become less self-evident to policy makers and they have become more difficult to defend. The momentum of the early period of reform has slowed and some earlier feminist gains have been lost. With the rise of post-industrial economies, and the growth of part-time, casual and increasingly mobile labour force (particularly in the service sector), and the breakdown of old class identities, men and women have been called upon to 'reinvent' themselves and develop new emotional lives (Walkerdine *et al.*, 2001). People are urged to 'get in touch with their true feelings', to recognise their limitations and potentialities, and to become 'emotionally literate' (see Chapter 5). This has been the context for the resurgence of biological, particularly genetic, explanations of difference.

Social constructionism has no doubt contributed significantly to a shift in thinking about difference, gender, and emotion. It has led to novel questions and encouraged new ways of thinking about old issues. However, scholars who undertake research from a social construc-tionist perspective often do not explicitly address issues of power and the politics of knowledge. The term 'social constructionism' covers a diverse range of approaches with contributions from scholars from many disciplines and with many different political commitments and orienta-tions. As Hacking (1999: 6–7) argues, social constructionists tend to be critical of the status quo insofar as the implication is that that which is socially constructed is not inevitable and that the social events, forces, and history which brought the social construction into being could well have been different (see Chapter 2). However, beyond a broad level of agreement that 'reality' is constructed, and about the fact that things could have been different, there are many versions of social constructionism, not all of which offer explicit, or particularly sophis-ticated, views on power and the politics of knowledge or insight into the construction of the *idea* of 'difference', whether 'constructed' or 'natural' (see Chapter 2). The currently fashionable idea that *both* 'nature' and 'culture' contribute to the formation of difference, advanced by many contemporary social scientists, begs for critical analysis. Such a claim is a convenient political compromise to those on either side of the 'nature'/'nurture' debate, but does little to clarify how behaviours, emotions, dispositions, and so on, come to be defined as having 'natural' and 'socially constructed' components. What scholarly research urgently needs is not more empirical evidence of the contributions of 'nature' and 'nurture' to the development of differences of sex/gender as though the issue could be resolved 'once and for all' by reference to a supposedly objective science, but rather new ways of thinking about the production and regulation of 'difference'. In particular, greater consideration needs to be given to the historical and socio-political contexts which shape ideas about the role of 'nature' and 'society' in determinating identities.

References to 'nature' or biology in discussions about emotional, intellectual, and physical difference have a long history. As Oudshoorn (1994), Schiebinger (1989), and other writers have argued, hormonal, anatomical, and other theories of 'essential' biological difference have been pervasive in the modern West, and have been used to justify women's subordination to men, both in the home and in the public domain. While one can trace the origins of the view that there are 'natural' differences between men and women, both in intellect and in character, as far back as the ancient Greeks, the authority of 'nature' in explanation has steadily increased since the late seventeenth century (Daston, 1996: 170–171). As the rise of liberal democracies promised new freedoms for men and women, many authors were proposing that there existed a different female intellect and that 'weakness' was a key attribute of the feminine character, intellect, and social situation (1996: 173–175). This difference was seen as rooted in reproductive difference, and other aspects of anatomy, which defined functions and determined intellectual development and emotional qualities. The notion of two different, but complementary 'sexes', which provided the epistemological foundation for noted social differences, gained credence in the eighteenth century, overturning the pre-Enlightenment 'one-sex' model in which the female was seen as the anatomical (and inferior) inversion of the male (Laqueur, 1990). The notion that men and women have different emotional experiences mirrors the conception of two anatomically distinct, but complementary sexes. Ideas of sexual attraction, affection, and romantic love have been premised upon this notion of complementarity, which denies other possible and existing configurations of sex, gender, sexual coupling, and sexual identity. What we take to be the 'normal' behaviours, outlooks, and experiences of men and women, respectively, is strongly linked to dualistic conceptions of sex and gender. It is no coincidence that the identity term 'the heterosexual' emerged at the very same historical point as 'the homosexual' (Katz, 1995). These categories are so taken for granted that commentators often overlook the fact that they are historically quite recent – dating from the late 1860s – and are by no means 'natural'. They reflect a normative ideal of identity and social relationships that has been recently subject to considerable scrutiny in the social sciences and humanities.

The question of difference and how it is conceived and described is central to contemporary debates in the social sciences and humanities, and is crucial in wider discussions about issues such as ethnicity, religion, and territorial affiliation. Language is obviously of profound significance in discussions about difference, since words import particular metaphors and associations, inviting certain interpretations and actions. Hence, the issue of how language is employed to construct difference is a recurring theme in this book. Labels are important, in defining objects, behaviours, dispositions, and so on, and in drawing distinctions from imagined 'others', and thus in establishing orientations for action. They can serve in a positive, affirming sense, to define a 'sense of self', to signify uniqueness and that which is to be valued, or in a negative, condemnatory way, to draw a distinction from, and to create, a foreign and feared 'other'. The context in which language is used is always important, as is the speaker(s), in giving meaning and significance to that that is signified. The word 'queer' began to be used in the 1980s and 1990s by people seeking to affirm a non-normative sexual identity, reversing the earlier use of this term by 'heterosexuals' to denigrate and control 'homosexuals' (Stein and Plummer, 1996: 134). US President Bush's use of term the 'evil axis' in 2002 to refer to countries with regimes that are seen to pose a threat to US interests created a self/other dichotomy and served as a powerful rhetorical device in the effort to mobilise action against a 'dangerous other'. In times of war, or when countries are preparing for war, it is common to demonise or dehumanise the 'other' in this way, in order to invoke fear among the population that is seen as necessary to legitimise military intervention. To describe someone or some group as 'aggressive', a term that is strongly coded 'masculine', for example, signifies a capacity for certain kinds of dangerous, usually 'outer-directed' behaviour, which is in need of control, harnessing, or evasive action, depending on the context. Similarly, to posit someone as 'depressed', which is strongly coded 'feminine' is to suggest an 'inner-directed' orientation, and perhaps the need for therapeutic intervention. As mentioned, 'emotion' is strongly associated with the feminine, and is seen as in need of control. Thus, policies which are premised on, for example, the assumption that men are 'naturally aggressive', or that women are more prone to 'depression' need careful scrutiny for what they imply for social policies and practices. In the past, the assumption that women were prone to irrational outbursts ('hysteria'), and that this was linked to their reproductive organs led to highly intrusive and repressive forms of intervention into women's bodies and lives; for example, clitoridectomies and incarceration. The figure of a 'hysterical' woman, who was nervous, and subject to an uncontrollable sexuality, and thus in need of medical control, appears in a number of histories (e.g. Ehrenreich and English, 1979; Foucault, 1980).

The influence of Darwinism on thinking about difference

Since the late nineteenth century, Darwinism has provided the dominant language and metaphors for describing and visualising sex/gender difference in many areas of behaviour and experience, including emotional expression and experience. The notions of instinct, evolution, and 'survival of the fittest' have served as shorthand terms to designate capacities and processes that are 'natural' and oriented to the survival of the organism, and hence difficult and even dangerous to change. The notion that men are naturally competitive and aggressive, pervasive in many contemporary societies, has long served to legitimise war and young men's involvement in combat, as well as to explain male dominance in public life. Military training has made extensive use of psychological theories, especially instinct theory, in disciplining men to kill and in making them effective fighters (Bourke, 1999: 93–102) (see Chapter 3).

Differences in sexual conduct has been explained and justified by reference to evolutionary theory. The notion that men have deep-seated urges or 'sex drives' oriented to the perpetuation of the species is common in popular discourse, and also informs some academic research and media portrayals on acts of male violence such as rape (see Chapter 4). Often such work is based on the study of non-human species. For example, Randy Thornhill and Craig Palmer, in their book, *A Natural History of Rape* (2000) rely on evidence from the study of scorpion flies, in arguing that rape represents the last resort of a frustrated male intent on continuing his genes. Dismissing social science explanations for rape for their supposed ideological bias and 'failure to generate cumulative scientific knowledge', Thornhill and Palmer draw on Darwin's theory of the role of sexual selection in evolution to answer the question, 'Why are males the rapists and females (usually) the victims?' They argue that 'selection favoured different adaptations of the sexes', which in turn 'is governed by the relative parental investment of the sexes'.

> Parental investment consists of the parental materials and services that determine the number and the survival of offspring; thus, it is the commodity for which each sex competes in the competition for mates. In humans, the parental investments of the two sexes may sometimes be nearly equal; however, the minimum parental investment for offspring by the male is trivial: a few minutes of mating and the small amount of energy needed to place an ejaculate in the female's reproductive tract. The female must invest all the time and energy required for gestation, birth, and lactation. The sex difference in the minimum parental investment is the key to understanding the sex-specific historical selection that gave rise to rape. Given the small investment of males and thus the low cost of each male mating, sexual selection favored males who achieved high mate numbers. As a result, men show greater interest than women in a variety of sexual partners and in casual sex without investment or commitment. Selection on females favored careful mate choice that allowed them to expend their precious parental investment under the circumstances most conducive to the production of viable offspring...Human rape arises from men's evolved machinery for obtaining a high number of mates in an environment where females choose mates. If men pursued mating only within committed relationships, or if women did not discriminate among potential mates, there would be no rape... (Thornhill and Palmer, 2000: 190–191)

Darwin himself contributed some ideas on sex differences, observing that while females may by default inherit some selected characteristics in relation to physical development and strength, 'vigor of intellect', beauty and 'strength of feeling', 'the masculine force always predominates' (Fausto-Stirling, 2000: 174). As I argue in Chapter 2, instinct theory has informed a great deal of psychology, particularly during its formative stages; for example the work of Havelock Ellis in his multi-volume, *Studies in the Psychology of Sex*. Following Darwin, evolutionary psychologists have argued that females have evolved to be more sexually reserved than men, and that this can explain problems in communication between the sexes, for example, confusion about sexual harassment (Fausto-Stirling, 2000: 175–176). Versions of evolutionary theory have been used to argue that women will never break through the 'glass ceiling' because, unlike men, they are not 'hard-wired' to be ambitious and to take risks, and that affirmative action will result in the hiring or promoting of inferior candidates (Fausto-Stirling, 2000: 176). Arguments that women are unable to compete on equal terms in the workplace often draw on ideas deriving from evolutionary psychology and neuroscience. An example is Moir and Jessel's (1991) claim that today's woman 'is personally and biologically disinclined' to compete and 'is further burdened by a sense of guilt and failure as a woman, a careerist, and a mother'. According to Moir and Moir, 'her mind, with its greater sensitivity to personal and moral aspects' puts her in perpetual conflict with the goals and values of 'the "masculine" ethos of management' (1991: 166–168). The view, expressed here, that women are sensitive to personal and moral issues that puts them in conflict with 'masculine' ways of thinking and acting, is shared by many scholars and lay publics alike and is sometimes presented as a virtue to be exploited. The often-unstated implication of such arguments is that women would be best advised not to bother attempting to compete with men in 'their' domain.

The assumption that there is a 'hard-wired' sex or gender difference in emotional disposition and response is pervasive in scholarly research, policy, and popular discourse. There are many versions of the 'hard-wired' account of difference, some making reference to hormones, some to brain chemistry or structure, and some to genetics (see, e.g. Badinter, 1995; Baron-Cohen, 2003; Moir and Moir, 1998; Moir and Jessel, 1991; Pease and Pease, 2001). However, despite differences in perspective, virtually all accounts assume a stable and dualistic sex/gender system, whereby two constructed 'genders' are founded on the bedrock of two biologically distinct, but complementary 'sexes'.

Both the two-sex/two-gender model and the notion of 'natural' or 'hard-wired' differences have widespread political appeal during a period of rapid economic, political, and social change. Historically, biological theories of difference, including gender and 'race' difference, have achieved particular prominence during periods of profound economic change, and have been used to justify the regulation, exclusion and persecution of certain groups – women, homosexuals, the mentally ill, the physically disabled, and non-Europeans (e.g. Allen, 1996, 1999; Guillaumin, 1995: 29–107). The emergence of the genetic worldview, described by Miringoff (1991) has paralleled the decline of the welfare state and increasing attacks on the rights of women and marginalised minority groups.

The rise of the concept of Genetic Welfare reflects the notion that the public good is best served not by social change but by biological intervention. As Miringoff argues, this has led to a shift in the conception of people's rights, duties, and responsibilities. Whereas Social Welfare was based on the assumption that people had a *right* to support, training, and rehabilitation, Genetic Welfare is based on the premise that people have a *duty* to play their part in advancing community health and well-being, and eliminating genetic abnormality, as responsible citizens and parents. They should do this by taking advantage of new genetic technologies to detect disease and prevent illness (Miringoff, 1991: 29–30). While Miringoff's argument pertains mainly to issues of genetic health, and the use of genetic screening by parents, increasingly, there has been reference to the genetic basis of sex/gender differences of all kinds, including emotional differences. This is reflected, for example, in articles in 'popular' science journals published in the 1980s and 1990s (Petersen, 1999). The implication behind the assumption that health and social problems, and behaviours and responses are genetically 'programmed' is that social interventions will be ineffective and that only therapeutic interventions are likely to be 'successful'.

The decline of the welfare state and the extension of market rationality to increasing areas of social life has been accompanied by the growing expectation that individuals, communities, and families, and particularly women, will take major responsibility for health and social care. The clear message is that no longer can citizens rely upon the state for social provision and to assume a social 'safety net', such as support during times of unemployment. The areas of health, education, social security, and unemployment provision are all increasingly oriented to creating self-sufficient, productive, enterprising citizens who will take charge of their own lives and become less reliant on the state. More and more, individuals are expected to take greater responsibility for self-care and care for others, in the community and the home. Programmes of 'care in the community', for example in the field of mental health care, and new systems of support for home-based carers, have followed in the wake of the scaling back or privatisation of state services. Often presented in the guise of strategies of 'community empowerment' or 'community participation', these programmes have sought to hand responsibility for care to those who are seen as 'naturally' inclined to care – namely women. This is occurring at the very same time that women are entering education and paid employment in growing numbers and making demands on the very services that were being 'rationed' or 'outsourced', such as childcare. It is argued that a woman's 'proper place' is in the home, as homemaker and carer and the expectation is that, if she works outside the home, she will work a 'double shift'. As I argue in Chapter 5, the emotional division of labour mirrors the physical division of labour, with women being especially vulnerable to exploitation of their labours.

What is often viewed as an enduring and 'natural' division of labour – the dualism of the roles of 'male breadwinner' and the unpaid 'homemaker' – is in fact a relatively recent 'invention'. A point frequently overlooked in debate about women's and men's 'natural roles' is that when factory work began in Britain, women and children were the predominant wage-labourers (Bittman and Pixley, 1997: 223). Across all OECD countries, the idea of a timeless and universal split between the dependent 'homemaker' and the 'breadwinner' was widespread only between 1890 and 1940. Since the 1940s, there has been a steady increase in women's participation in the workforce. Nevertheless, policies pertaining to the family, including the 'family wage' and unemployment benefits, have been premised upon the 'breadwinner'/dependent 'homemaker' split (Bittman and Pixley, 1997: 214–225; Edley and Wetherell, 1996: 107). This reflects the liberal doctrine of separate public and private spheres, with women's 'proper place' assumed to be in the home in a caring, supportive role (Bittman and Pixley, 1997: 224–230). The notion of separate spheres is fully consistent with the aforementioned idea of complementary 'sexes'; that is, women and men have minds and dispositions that are different, but complementary (see also Chapter 2). Although this ideal has been held to provide the foundation for a harmonious, 'workable', marriage and relationship, in practice it has buttressed male domination and women's exclusion from the public realm (Lloyd, 1984: 76). A further point that is often overlooked in discussions is that this complementary schema embodies a heterosexist bias in that it denies associations of emotional experience and expression and sex that do not conform to those prescribed by normative hetero-sexuality; for example, romantic love (see Chapter 4). One of the aims of this book will be to show how the idea of two gender-distinctive spheres of emotional experience and expression serves to privilege particular kinds of social and sexual relations.

Equality versus 'celebration of difference' arguments

There has long been a tension in feminism between those 'schools' which deny an 'essential' sex/gender difference and those who affirm, indeed celebrate, difference. While some feminists argue that the political goal for women should be assimilation (i.e. achieving power and participation on equal terms with men in dominant institutions), others contend that it is important to organise autono-mously and assert a positive group cultural identity based on particular 'feminine' attributes or qualities (Young, 1990: 158–164). Those who deny an 'essential' difference (the so-called equality or egalitarian feminists) seek to create mechanisms for equal opportunity and women's greater involvement in spheres of activity traditionally defined as 'masculine', particularly the world of paid work. For example, noted differences in women's representation in senior management, science, engineering, and academe is seen as a consequence of a masculine bias in education and in workplaces which deters women from pursuing careers in these areas and creates a 'glass ceiling' inhibiting promotion to the senior positions. Equal opportunities and affirmative action policies are premised on the assumption that there are social structural impediments to women's (and minority ethnic groups') advancement that need to be overcome. Feminists who acknowledge and celebrate difference (sometimes called 'difference' feminists), on the other hand, seek to promote the positive character-istics of the uniquely feminine to counter masculine values and ways of relating; for example, empathy, care for the other, listening skills, and non-competitiveness. Some strands of eco-feminism, for example, assert that women are 'closer' to the biological and natural processes of birth and child-rearing and therefore embody the relational capacities required to sustain 'nature' and engender peace (Petersen, 1998: 84) (see Chapter 3).

'Difference' feminism developed in part as a response of the perceived failures of equality feminism. It is argued that, while the ideal of liberation has brought significant improvement in the status of women and minority groups, the achievement of formal equality has not eliminated social differences (see, e.g. Young, 1990: 164). In Young's view, there is a need for a more contextualised and relational understanding of difference, which recognises that 'Different groups are always similar in some respects, and always potentially share some attributes, experiences and goals' (Young, 1990: 171). Others, however, contend that the failure of equality feminism has been the failure of scholars and activists to recognise basic biological differences between the sexes, including differences in abilities (e.g. perceptual, attentive, verbal, visual-spatial, numerical), competitiveness, parenting, level of sexual interest, patterns of communication, leadership, and metabolism (see, e.g. Moir and Moir, 1998; Payne, 2001; Tooley, 2002). Drawing on scientific studies of sex differences to support their arguments, a number of writers have sought to put their case as to 'why the sexes can't be equal'.

In his book, *The Miseducation of Women*, James Tooley (2002) asserts that efforts to achieve equality between the sexes is 'bad' for woman in that it denies 'women's ways of knowing' and their access to those endeavours to which women are especially qualified. Gender stereotyping, the target of egalitarian feminists and educational reformers, Tooley argues, should be celebrated rather than denigrated (e.g. Tooley, 2002: 27–39, 42). Tooley draws on the ideas of evolutionary psychology to account for the supposed failures in educational reform and women's alleged continuing unhappiness. 'Equality feminism' is a particular target of Tooley's criticism: its failure to acknowledge women's preferences for 'feminine' subjects over 'masculine ones, and the denial of 'feminine ways of knowing'. In his view,

> we would create a better, more just society if we could promote these feminine ways of knowing and approaches in schools and society at large, and if we could recognise 'connectedness, as much

as independence', feminine ways as much as masculine ways. It would be more just for girls if these alternative ways of knowing were made available and more valued in the school curriculum. (2002: 37)

Another variant of this difference argument is posited by Moir and Moir (1998). The authors refer to findings from research on the biochemistry of the brain to argue that 'many men are 'neurologically driven to risk' and to 'play to win', and that women's neurochemistry makes them more 'risk averse'. This biological difference is seen to lead to misunderstanding between the sexes and to have a profound impact on working lives and careers (1998: Chapter 5). In Moir and Moir's view, men excel more often in the area of paid work because their brain makes them more 'capable of a much narrower focus'. The authors refer to research on the brain that shows how 'the male shuts down parts of his brain so that another area can concentrate on a problem, while a female keeps both hemispheres working during the problem's solution'. The female, it seems, is more distracted, for example by 'worries about her family and friends, while a man will ruthlessly let both go while he completes the task' (1998: 180). However, with an increasing number of women entering the workforce, which employers have discovered are 'less argumentative, more co-operative, more flexible in their hours... and will accept lower pay', men are being displaced from many of the lower status jobs, creating 'damaged' men and a 'male underclass' (1998: 180–181, 196). As Moir and Moir argue, 'Men and women who are successful in job areas that are usually the preserve of the opposite sex come from the tiny proportion of the population in whom the hormonal balance was upset during the foetal stage'. 'They are not pioneers for a brave new world, but exceptions to the biological rule' (1998: 188).

Like Tooley, Moir and Moir see equal opportunities policies as having failed to create equal representation in different areas and levels of work – a failure that can be explained by biology (1998: 193). They argue that 'the demand that a man get in touch with his emotions [to create a better world] is sheer psychobabble for, unless he is dead, a man is already in complete touch with them. It just so happens that his emotions are not hers' (1998: 256). Differences in brain 'networks' mean that men are more easily able to compartmentalise their emotions and less able to express their feelings. As Moir and

Moir argue, the 'emotional silence [of men] frequently persuades women that men are insensitive, and in many ways they are quite right. Men are genuinely less sensitive than women' (1998: 259). As they go on to say, 'He does not like "confusing" issues with emotional factors, preferring a swift, concrete solution, while she will take everyone's feelings into consideration.' This is because 'his brain is not equipped to make links across the complex emotional field, and she reads emotional cues far better than he does (if he reads them at all)' (1998: 263). Further, men hate talking about their feelings, preferring instead to show their emotions by actions rather than by words and any attempt by a female partner to 'open up' only creates anger. Men's emotional distance is 'one of the hardest things for a woman to understand', yet is preordained by biology, and is a way in which men seek to control their ever-present fear of testosterone-fuelled violent emotions (1998: 265–268).

One can discern common threads in recent books such as the above, including the identification of mutually exclusive and irreconcilable sex differences, reference to biological (particularly evolutionary) arguments and evidence, and the appeal for recognition, if not celebration, of discrete gender qualities, emotions, and dispositions. Such arguments have been used to justify women's exclusion from the public sphere, particularly full participation in paid work, and to explain men's violent behaviour. Significantly, such literature has emerged during a period of rapid change, involving a retreat from social welfare provision and changes in the nature of the employment and a questioning of gender roles. The notion that women are 'essentially' different, but equal, and/or that society should be celebrating difference serves to legitimate policies of unequal treatment, in particular women's exclusion from domains of social life traditionally dominated by men, and to reinforce structures of domination. It is noteworthy that few of these texts make reference to issues of power, or to historical and social science evidence undermining the argument for an 'essential', timeless, natural difference between men and women. Critical scholarship, particularly work questioning the immutability of 'nature', 'biology', and 'difference' is either ignored or rejected out of hand. For example, Moir and Moir dismiss critical academic contributions, which they crudely characterise as 'postmodernism' (1998: 13–20).

The recent 'discovery' of the emotions in sociology and the development of new perspectives in gender studies provide the opportunity for posing new questions about gender and emotion: for example, what is at stake in prevailing gender–emotion associations? What are the broad economic, political, and global implications of these associations? How do men and women enact gender scripts and to what extent do they subscribe to the 'rules of feeling' that attach to their gender? And, what are the prospects for developing new constructions of gender and emotion? This book endeavours to help shift the terms of the debate about gender-based emotional differences, to challenge the reductionist and dualistic thinking that has characterised this field of analysis thus far, and to map new pathways for research and action. It is hoped that in disrupting that which appears so self-evident, enduring, indeed 'prescribed by nature', namely gender differences in emotionality, this book will contribute to the rethinking of gender and emotion and to the effort to create a more just society.

Outline of remaining chapters

Chapter 2 directs attention to psychology, a field of study and practice that, as mentioned, has profoundly shaped thinking about sex/gender difference. Making specific reference to the psychology of aggression, it shows how ideas about natural difference are manifested in theories. As I argue, the psychology of aggression reveals the profound influence of Darwinism, especially in instinct theories and notions of innateness. The legacy of Darwin, it is argued, is clearly evident in the increasingly influential field of evolutionary psychology, which views sex differences in aggression as adaptive. However, as I show, throughout its history, psychology theories of aggression have reflected the assumption that men are 'naturally' more aggressive than women – an assumption which is evident even in learning theory which, on the face of it, would seem to question the idea of innateness. The chapter concludes by examining the challenge posed to the psychology of emotion by the recent turn in the social sciences to social constructionism. It considers some problems with work undertaken by those adopting this approach thus far and draws attention to scholars' lack of reflection on how psychology constructs its categories of analysis.

Chapter 3 explores the significance of the military and warfare as contexts for engendering emotions. The links between gender and emotion are perhaps nowhere more evident than in the institutions of the military and the theatres of war. Debates about women's involvement in combat roles and popular cultural portrayals of the male warrior rely upon generalised depictions of men's and women's emotional make-ups. Focusing on some influential and recent texts on the origins of war, the chapter begins by exploring some enduring beliefs about gender, aggression, and war. The idea that war is a result of innate or instinctual aggression in 'man' has been a dominant theme in the literature, again reflecting the influence of Darwin, as well as Freud. The chapter examines the role of the news media as a source for images of the links between gender, emotion, and war. The potential of the media to shape public views on international conflict in general, and on the links between masculinity, aggression, and war, in particular, was emphasised during the Gulf War of 2003. I examine how women have been portrayed in the context of the military and assess claims about women's innate difference in capacity for aggression, as well as claims about the potential of women to disrupt all male groups, which have justified women's exclusion from combat roles. I also explore the role played by military training and the use of language in engendering difference. Finally, I consider the extent to which the changing character of war, wrought by new global forces and formations and new technologies, unsettles established ideas on gender and emotion.

Chapter 4 turns to the analysis of the links between love, intimacy, and sex, and asks whether recent apparent shifts in the discourse of romantic love and in sexual rituals represent a challenge to constructions of gender difference. The chapter explores the role of expertise in generating knowledge about love and sex, and a growing consumerist orientation in matters of the heart. It begins by examining the discourses of romantic love which have dominated views on 'normal' intimate relations between 'the sexes' in the West since the late eighteenth century. Recent scholarship has highlighted the variable meanings and socio-political implications of 'romantic love'. The social constructionist idea that love is an *accomplishment* that presupposes interacting persons directs attention to the practices of love. The chapter explores the origins of the notion of romantic or passionate love as an irrational force – an overwhelming attraction for the other – and the construction of the link between 'falling in love' and 'making love'. It also examines challenges to, and changes in, the Romantic ideal. It then turns to the contemporary period and examines some emergent practices such as online dating and 'speed dating' and asks whether they signify a change in gender norms and relations. I argue that, despite evidence of recent shifts in the norms governing intimate relationships, and an increasingly consumerist orientation to matters of the heart, the romantic ideal continues to exert a powerful influence on thinking about sex/gender differences. Finally, the chapter examines how the notion of complementary difference in the sphere of love, intimacy, and sex, and the public/private distinction, serve in the gender division of emotional and sexual labour.

Finally, Chapter 5 investigates some implications for the concepts of gender and gender difference of the recent focus on emotionality and 'emotional literacy' in a number of contemporary societies. According to its proponents, 'emotional literacy' promises a range of benefits for the individual and society, including improved health and social relationships, reduced school dropout rates, and less aggressive and destructive behaviour. A range of new policies and programmes, focusing on schools, workplaces, and community settings, have aimed to raise levels of 'emotional literacy'. Many of these initiatives have been directed specifically at men and boys. This chapter examines the politics of 'emotional literacy' and uncovers underlying gender biases and conceptions of self in recent literature. As I argue, the growing emphasis on 'emotional literacy' may be explained by the particular significance attributed to emotional labour, or at least particular kinds of emotional labour, in late capitalist societies. The chapter explores the implications for the gendered division of labour of the growing commodification of emotion. The therapeutic emphasis of 'emotional literacy' policies and programmes serves to divert attention from the substantial economic, social, and political issues at stake in the definition of problems as having an 'emotional' basis. Finally, to conclude the chapter and the book, I explore how current categories and dualisms have constrained thought about gender and emotion, and identify some areas where critical studies may help affect change in thinking and practice; namely, in science, the media, and law. I finish by arguing for a more explicitly 'emotion-focused' gender studies and for greater attention to the politics of 'emotion'.

2
Psychology, Gender, and Emotion

As noted, psychology has been a key discipline in the study of sex or gender differences in emotional experience and expression. An entire sub-field of psychology has in fact been devoted to the study and measurement of such differences. The psychology of sex/gender differences is often seen to begin with the publication of Maccoby and Jacklin's *The Psychology of Sex Differences* (1974). However, psychological research on gender differences can be traced back further, to the late nineteenth century and the origins of psychology itself (Hyde and Mezulis, 2001: 552). Debates since then have focused centrally on the issue of whether or not noted differences are 'significant', usually meant in a statistical sense. The question of 'significance' is difficult to resolve since this is ultimately a question of one's values and commitment to particular perspectives and methods. In the same way as 'intelligence' is a product of intelligence tests, 'difference' is an artefact of the particular theories and methods adopted. Despite efforts to produce value-free accounts of difference, it is not possible for researchers to set aside their values, which will influence their conception of 'difference' and their interpretation of its 'significance'. Assumptions about 'essential' differences are deeply entrenched in the history and the theories and practices of the discipline of psychology. In this chapter, I examine the nature of these assumptions and how they are manifest in various psychological theories of sex/gender and emotion.

In their wide-ranging and pioneering review of a large body of evidence bearing on sex differences, drawn from such areas as perception, learning, memory, intellectual abilities, cognitive styles,

and temperament, Maccoby and Jacklin (1974) found 'some peculi-
arities of interpretation of data, distortions that occur frequently
enough to deserve comment'. For example, they found that writers
often refer to 'studies that included subjects of only one sex as if they
had demonstrated a sex difference' (1974: 6). As they observed, 'sex
stereotyping' about the behaviour expected of each sex 'runs deep'
and that 'even when sex differences are incidental to the main focus
of the study, the observers must almost inevitably be biased to
some extent' (1974: 7). According to Maccoby and Jacklin, there is
a tendency for some researchers to ignore evidence that did not fit
with preconceptions about difference or lack of difference. They cited
'instances in which there has been direct pressure to keep findings out
of the published literature when they do not agree with the accepted
view of some process or relationship' (1974: 4). They commented
that, 'it is our impression that there is a substantial primacy effect in
beliefs about scientific truths – that it takes a great deal of evidence to
refute an original erroneous impression' (1974: 12). Their conclusion
was that, although there appeared to be some differences in some
abilities and dispositions, most notably in aggression, there existed
a number of 'unfounded beliefs about sex differences' or insufficient
evidence to support a belief about difference (1974: 349–355). More
recently, other writers have also drawn attention to stereotyping in
studies of sex differences (e.g. Canary and Emmers-Sommer,
1997: 23) and noted that, insofar as differences are observed, these
are small in absolute terms (Manstead, 1998: 236–237).

Since the publication of Maccoby and Jacklin's study, work on sex/
gender differences has shown no sign of diminishing, with recent
literature addressing such topics such as gender differences in emotionality, communication, disposition, and behaviour (see, e.g. Fischer,
2000; Worell, 2001). Given the potential for such work to reinforce
power relations, to bolster arguments that men and women are
fundamentally different and therefore should be treated unequally,
a number of writers have recently wondered whether psychologists
should study sex or gender differences at all (e.g. Eagly, 1995; Hyde
and Mezulis, 2001: 553). This is a vexed question, which can be
answered either in the affirmative or negative according to one's
view on the history of the discipline and belief in the power and
value of scientific knowledge. In seeking to cast light on this issue,
this chapter examines how psychology through its knowledge and

practices contributes to our understanding of sex/gender differences in emotionality. Drawing in particular from the field of the psychology of aggression, an area where sex/gender differences are seen by many writers to be especially prominent, it shows how ideas about natural differences have informed debates about emotion, demonstrating the enduring influence of Darwinism. In recent years, a growing body of critical literature has drawn attention to the value-laden nature and politics of psychological knowledge, some of which will be reviewed in the following paragraphs.

Psychology as discourse and practice

Psychological research has a great deal of credibility among many sections of the population, including influential decision makers, and currently enjoys high status in the human sciences. Psychologists are often consulted by those developing policies and by the media for their views on human behaviour and for insights into the workings of the human mind. There is currently a wave of public interest in psychology, particularly explorations of sex or gender differences, as evidenced by a burgeoning number of popular psychology books and journals in this area. Psychology is presented by its practitioners as a disinterested field of enquiry that produces objective knowledge and is largely untainted by the ideologies and value commitments that infect the other 'soft' human sciences, such as anthropology and sociology. Psychologists are widely seen, and tend to portray themselves as 'scientists of the mind'. Many academic psychologists identify themselves as natural scientists rather than social scientists, and academic departments of psychology are often located in faculties of science rather than social science. Although many psychologists like to present themselves as disinterested scientists or practitioners, recent historical and critical social science scholarship has revealed psychology's value biases and its role in political projects oriented to the regulation of self and society. Psychologists in the main have been disinclined to critically reflect upon the value biases of their work and to examine the social and political implications of their particular ways of understanding the world. Any adequate understanding of the construction of gender differences in emotionality in contemporary society must recognise the central role played by psychology in shaping cultural knowledge about difference and 'normal' identity.

In his book, *Governing the Soul* (1989), Nikolas Rose has documented the various ways in which psychology has been deployed during the twentieth century to shape the private self. In work, war, childhood socialisation, and intimate relationships, psychology has offered the perspectives and tools for producing productive, self-regulating subjects, and rectifying the 'maladjustments' of conduct that threaten to disrupt the social order. Many psychological tools, such as intelligence testing, employed in periods of war and peace have transformed our ways of thinking about and organising human affairs within military and 'civilian' contexts. In the next and later chapters, I examine in more detail some of the ways in which psychological knowledge has been deployed for shaping our thinking in these contexts. Far from being objective measures of our inner mental states, psychological tests have offered a new way of visualising normality and difference, and producing citizens who display certain mental capacities, dispositions, and moral attributes (Rose, 1989: Chapter 12). As Rose argues elsewhere, psychology can be thought of as more than 'merely a theoretical discipline'. It comprises an assortment of 'ways of thinking and acting, practices, techniques, forms of calculation, routines and procedures, and skilled personnel', and is linked strategically to other discourses such as criminology, political philosophy, statistics, medicine, and psychiatry (Rose, 1996: 104). It serves as a crucial link between biological discourse and other discourses that speak to the individual (Venn, 1984: 127). It has produced new domains of supposedly objective knowledge, allowing us to think old things anew while making 'new things thinkable and practicable' (Rose, 1996: 105). While psychologists tend to portray psychology as an objective study of the psyche, consciousness, human mental life, and so on – critical scholars have shown that its truths are inescapably 'social'. Psychology as a social practice constitutes the objects that it seeks to know (Rose, 1996: 107–108). According to Rose, techniques such as 'statistics' and 'the experiment' have been important tools or methods within psychology for establishing a regime of truth about persons, and for improving the capacity of different groups to understand their own actions and regulate their own conduct. The images, values, vocabularies, and techniques have become indispensable resources for individuals for acting upon their bodies and minds, so as to transform themselves into ethical beings and to achieve autonomy (Rose, 1996: 111–122).

Psychology and the study of sex/gender difference

Psychology plays a key role in the formation of beliefs about sex/gender and difference through its implicit assumptions about 'normal' rational behaviour and sexuality, and through the promotion of concepts and theories pertaining to sex/gender difference (e.g. sex instincts, the 'male sex drive', gender socialisation). Notions of normality are embodied in statistical measures and psychological testing, which take for granted the specific conception of the individual as a unitary rational male subject (Venn, 1984: 131). As Venn argues, psychology owes its focus on the study of the normal – and on deviation, pathology, and error – to the new biology inaugurated by the Darwinian revolution. Psychology is in the main concerned with the calibration of error or 'deviation from the norm', rather than with questioning the normality of the norm itself (Venn, 1984: 131). Although some recent critical strands of psychology do question the norm and analyse how it is formed and sustained, such work is seen as marginal to the substantial concerns of the discipline. The focus on the norm in the psychology of sex differences can be traced back to the nineteenth century and the work of Darwin and his contemporaries (see Chapter 1).

Darwin's book, *The Descent of Man, and Selection in Relation to Sex*, published in 1871, provided the source for generation of research in evolutionary psychology and provided the starting point for a psychology of sex differences (Russett, 1989: 40). Although Darwin provided only an outline for such a field of study, the prestige of his name gave the field of sex differences research legitimacy and set the terms for subsequent discussion (Russett, 1989: 40). Drawing analogies from the animal kingdom, as was typical of the evolutionary argument, and one used extensively through *The Descent*, Darwin noted differences in temperament between men and women. Thus, men were seen as having courage, pugnacity, energy, and excelling in qualities such as abstraction, reason, and imagination. Women, on the other hand, were seen to have greater powers of intuition, rapid perception, tenderness, and perhaps imitation (Russett, 1989: 40–41). As Russett notes, Darwin had little evidence of a sexual disparity in temperament, other than his own and others' observations of behaviour in the animal kingdom and among humans from other cultures. Although he employed a tentative tone in much of his discussion of temperamental differences, this tone disappeared when his discussion shifted to 'intellectual powers' proper, where it was clear to him that man attained 'higher eminence' in whatever he takes up – whether thought, reason, or imagination (Russett, 1989: 41). Here, he drew on the notion of 'the law of deviation from averages', recently developed by his cousin Francis Galton (the founder of eugenics) to support his case (1989: 41). Although Darwin's work on sex differences clearly had a profound influence on thinking on this field of study, it would be wrong to imply that he alone was responsible for generating the ideas which continue to hold sway over psychology and in areas of scholarship beyond this discipline. Others, too, around this time were beginning to contribute to a discourse of sex differences, making use of the notion of the norm to define an 'ideal' – implicitly coded masculine – from which deviation – implicitly, the feminine – could be established.

In these early writings, the notion of *instinct* was pervasive. As I shall explain, when I turn to the discussion of psychological theories of aggression, within the Darwinian worldview, the sex instinct was conceived as a 'driving' force – a fact reflected in many writings of the late nineteenth and early twentieth centuries. The individual is 'driven' by this instinct, whose ultimate goal is survival of the species. Ribot, when writing of love, expressed a view common among many writers of the late nineteenth and early twentieth centuries:

> At bottom, the irresistible element is in the sexual instinct, and only exists in virtue of it; instinctive activity alone has such power. This is what Schopenhauer calls, in metaphysical terms, the Genius of the species, which makes of the individual an instrument for the furtherance of its ends. We might also call it, in biological terms...the continuity of the germ-plasm which energetically manifests and affirms itself, safeguarding the rights of the species against individual fancies. But all these metaphors explain nothing, add nothing to the simple verification of the fact. Sexual instinct remains the centre round which everything revolves; nothing exists but through it... (Ribot, 1911: 256)

As this quotation illustrates so well, the sexual instinct is seen as a species-survival mechanism that overrides individual volition or wants. Individuals are *impelled* to play their part in reproduction, for the survival of the species. What is not spelt out here, but is clearly evident in other writings of the period as well as in contemporary evolutionary psychology, is the view that there are sex differences in the manifestation of this 'drive'. Men are generally seen as having a 'greater drive' than women, a difference often seen to explain men's greater aggressiveness or tendency to dominate women. According to what has been called the male sexual drive discourse (Hollway, 1984: 231), men's and women's sexualities are biologically 'programmed', the assumption being that such differences are not easily subject to change (see Chapter 1).

That there are different sexual 'drives' that are complementary is seen as a fact of 'nature' that functions for the survival of the species. Thus, women's supposed passivity in sexual encounters is often explained in terms of its complementary and functional role in reproduction. In his *Studies in the Psychology of Sex* (1925), Havelock Ellis, asked, 'What are the special characters of the sexual impulse in women?', to which he responded:

> There is certainly one purely natural sexual difference of a funda-
> mental character, which lies at the basis of whatever truth may be
> in the assertion that women are not susceptible of sexual emotion.
> As may be seen when considering the phenomena of modesty,
> the part played by the female in courtship throughout nature is
> usually different from that played by the male, and is, in some
> respects, a more difficult and complex part. Except when the male
> fails to play his part properly, she is usually comparatively passive;
> in the proper playing of her part she has to appear to shun the
> male, to flee from his approaches – even actually to repel them.
> Courtship resembles very closely, indeed, a drama or game; and
> the aggressiveness of the male, the coyness of the female, are alike
> unconsciously assumed in order to bring about in the most effectual
> manner the ultimate union of the sexes. The seeming reluctance
> of the female is not intended to inhibit sexual activity either in the
> male or in herself, but to increase it in both. The passivity of the
> female, therefore, is not real, but only an apparent, passivity, and
> this holds true of our own species as of the lower animals ... (Ellis,
> 1925: 228–229)

The notion of complementary sexual roles, such as in the courtship ritual, referred to here, has been central to the discourse of sexual difference. As Genevieve Lloyd argues in her book, *The Man of Reason:*

'Male' and 'Female' in Western Philosophy (1984), from the beginnings of philosophical thought, femaleness has been symbolically associated with what reason has excluded – sensuality, emotion, desire, embodied experience, and nature. However, beginning with the Enlightenment, philosophers began to see the minds of women and men as quite different in ways that made them 'complementary'. Such a view was compatible with ancient ideas of sex differences as well as with liberal democratic thought that was emerging from the late eighteenth century onwards. This supported the view that men and women were, 'by nature', different, but performed complementary roles. Thus, references to 'nature' or 'the lower animals', seen in the above quote, have been common. The supposed male 'aggressiveness' and female 'coyness' were seen as expressive of 'natural' instincts and thus outside conscious control. This view fitted neatly with the new liberal democratic order, with the emerging division of labour based upon gender-specific roles, with women as nurturers and mothers and men as paid workers and public citizens. The view of complementary opposites received support from anatomists, who depicted male and female bodies as perfect in their differences (e.g. Laqueur, 1990; Schiebinger, 1989), as well as psychologists, such as those above, who identified differences in reasoning, perception, and emotionality.

Instinct theory also influenced Freud's highly influential psychoanalytic account of sex socialisation as well as his ideas on civilisation and the repression of sexuality and 'aggressivity'. The development of dualistic gender roles can be explained by the dynamic interplay between biological impulses or 'drives', psychological processes, and social constraints. There is a constant tension between the unconscious desire for the immediate satisfaction of our drives (the pleasure principle), and the conscious acknowledgement of the need to modify this desire (the reality principle). Freud's work on gender socialisation emphasised the centrality of one's love and hate relationship with one's parents – the Oedipus complex – and its resolution to the development of differences in male and female psyches. In Freud's view, girls, unlike boys, failed to fully resolve the Oedipus complex and were thus destined to have a weaker conscience, or 'superego' (Stockard, 1999: 222). However, according to 'object-relations' theory, developed by Freud's followers, differences in gender socialisation is explained by boys' and girls' different relationships to their mothers and the difficulty for boys in learning to become male. Boys learn what is 'masculine' by rejecting and repressing the feminine; hence, boys' gender identity tends to become more tenuous than girls' identity (Stockard, 1999: 223). Freud's work and that of other psychoanalysts has been criticised by many feminists for its 'masculinist' bias, and for being ahistorical, acultural, and for rationalising the relations of domination and subordination between the sexes (Rowley and Grosz, 1990: 180–183). Object-relations theory has nevertheless had a significant impact on a number of areas of feminism, and has been the starting point for a number of influential theorists, including Nancy Chodorow, Juliet Mitchell, and Dorothy Dinnerstein, whose work focuses on analyses of mothering, child-rearing, and the acquisition of gender identity. According to these psychoanalytic accounts, men and women have different 'ways of relating' and notions of morality that can be directly traced to early childhood experiences of socialisation (e.g. Chodorow, 1978; Gilligan, 1982) (see Chapter 1). Although psychoanalysis offers a much more sophisticated explanation of gender difference than instinct theory, it can be criticised on a number of grounds, including its apparent imperviousness to contrary evidence (see, e.g. Dimen, 1995; Rutherford, 1992). Despite such criticisms, psychoanalysis currently enjoys widespread popularity and prestige outside academe, and provides a vehicle for conveying Darwinian ideas into the wider public domain.

Evolutionary psychology

Although Darwinian evolutionists have diverse views on sexual, racial and cultural difference, the terms 'Darwinian' and 'evolutionary' have been invoked to explain all kinds of processes, including psycho-logical processes (Rose and Rose, 2000: 1). Evolutionary psychology, which has development and found application in a growing number of areas in recent years, makes extensive reference to the adaptive advantage of various behaviours and preferences, drawing on evidence from the animal kingdom, as did earlier psychologists. According to one definition, 'evolutionary psychology is the application of evolutionary principles to the study of the evolution of the mind (Tooby and Cosmides, 1992, cited in Campbell, 2002: 8). As Campbell explains, evolutionary psychology is concerned with 'the mechanisms of the mind and not simply behaviour', which distinguishes it from sociobiology, where comparisons are made between animal and human behaviours and conclusions are drawn about common or convergent patterns of evolution under similar selection pressures (2002: 9). However, while evolutionary psychologists may claim that their primary concern is the mind rather than behaviour, behavioural comparisons tend to provide the starting point for locating the mental mechanisms that produce the behaviours – a Point in fact acknowledged by Campbell (2002: 9). Evolutionary Psychology's focus on species-specific adaptations to seek explanations for supposedly universal aspects of human experience leads its adherents to downplay the role of 'culture' and to look for evidence from 'nature'. Adaptation is seen, and described, as 'hard-wired', not for all time but over the longer period for which the behavioural or mental attribute is useful or 'functional' for the species. Evolutionary psychologists have also explained warfare as an adaptive strategy for acquiring resources that will allow mating so as to ensure the continuity of the species (Nelkin, 2000: 21). Campbell (2002) draws extensively on evidence from studies of primates and other animals, as well as data from criminal statistics, to support her argument for sex differences in aggression. In her view, 'male aggression was driven upwards by competition for mating opportunities', which makes males take more risks, whereas 'female competition was held in check by a mother's need to ensure her own survival and, with it, her reproductive investment' (2002: 64). Female 'restraint from aggression', she argues, can be explained by their greater fear, which is 'functional for females', 'restraining them from exposing themselves to unnecessary danger and from the possibility of sustaining injury or death that would have disastrous implications for their young' (2002: 94). Evolutionary psychologists have defended their approach as offering a 'true' account of sex differences (see, e.g. Campbell, 2002: 12–31), and often seem oblivious to the political implications of their work.

Within the framework of evolutionary psychology, virtually any behaviour, mental attribute, or disposition can be explained as having evolved as a consequence of its adaptive value, including those aspects of the mind which are seen by many to be 'quintessentially human', for example emotionality, culture, language, and the ability to reflect on one's actions (consciousness). According to Daniel Dennett, in his recent book, *Freedom Evolves* (2003), the ability to use language, and the associated thought processes, and to assimilate culture, makes humans unique in the animal kingdom; however, this capacity itself is part of our evolved biology. Thus understood, humans have the capacity to harness scientific knowledge to increase their choices, for example through the development of better medical treatments. The problem this highlights, and is common with evolutionary psychology, is the reliance on a teleological argument that is difficult, if not impossible, to refute on scientific grounds. That is, behaviours or mental processes are explained in terms of the ends towards which they are supposedly directed. Evolutionary psychology takes current social arrangements, and ways of thinking and acting, as given, and hence as necessarily useful or 'functional'. In relation to apparent gender differences in emotion, these are seen to serve a useful social purpose, and hence to have adaptive value. In the same way that functionalist social theorists explain social roles or patterns of social interaction in terms of the function they fulfil for the stability of society as a whole, evolutionary psychologists render mental processes intelligible in terms of their adaptive value for the species. There is little acknowledgement of the power relations that underlie current social arrangements and our ways of thinking and acting, or apparent recognition that things could be different. Evolutionary psychology offers a deeply conservative view of the world and provides evidence and arguments that can be used, and have been used, to justify all kinds of social inequalities and exploitative or hostile actions; for example, war, rape, and sexual exploitation.

During a period of rapid change, involving the retreat of the welfare state, and a questioning of long established narratives of progress (e.g. socialism) and of scientific development, and consequent increasing uncertainty, biological explanations, which seem to offer certainty, have great appeal (Rose and Rose, 2000: 3–4). However, although interest in biological explanations of difference has been especially prominent in recent years, there have been recurring references to innate or 'natural' differences in the history of psychological writings on emotion from the beginnings of the discipline. Some of the early theories may now seem quaint and to have been superseded by more sophisticated theories. However, some of the ideas continue to circulate in the broader culture and to influence thinking about gender and emotion, sometimes via the updated languages of genetics and neuroscience.

Sex differences in psychology's theories of aggression

Assumptions about a natural sex difference in propensity to aggress, with men being 'naturally more aggressive' than women, have been widespread in the history of psychology. These assumptions have been either explicit in formal theories of aggression, or implicit in the kinds of questions pursued, and the use of methodologies and supporting evidence. However, research on aggression has not been without its critics. The cross-cultural salience of categories used in research, such as 'aggression', and the view that behaviours, such as 'aggressivity', are sex-specific, has been questioned (see, e.g. Bjorkqvist and Niemela, 1992; Burbank, 1994; Harvey and Gow, 1994). Scholars have also challenged the assumption that aggressive or violent behaviours have a biological basis (see, e.g. Bleier, 1984: 94–101; Fausto-Stirling, 1992: 123–154). As critical scholars have indicated, psychologists have failed to adequately scrutinise the terms 'aggression' and 'aggressivity'. These terms are highly contentious, but theorists tend to assume that their meanings are self-evident. 'Aggression' is sometimes used in titles of research papers when the research being reported is of *fighting behaviour* between animals or people. In such cases, the use of language is not only imprecise, but may also be laden with anthropomorphic values and meanings (Bleier, 1984: 95). Fausto-Stirling has referred to the tendency of writers on aggression to confuse and interchange social and individual (or biological) concepts. For example, in some theories about the origins of war, *aggression* (an individual level phenomenon) is used interchangeably with *war* (a social level phenomenon) (1992: 129). Others have raised doubt about whether it is meaningful at all to debate whether one sex is more or less aggressive than another without taking into account the type of conflict (e.g. whether between groups or inter-personal), the parties involved (i.e. male–male, female–female or male–female), and the cultural context. It has been suggested that observed sex differences in levels of aggression may simply reflect the fact that men and women have different 'styles' or 'strategies' of aggressive behaviour which, in the event, are likely to vary according to context (Bjorkqvist, 1994; Burbank, 1994). Despite such criticisms, the idea that there is a 'natural' sex-based difference in aggression has continued to dominate psychological and popular thought, which is especially evident in discussions about the origins of warfare and the male role in combat (see Chapter 3). Many of our contemporary assumptions about natural sex differences began to emerge in the late nineteenth and early twentieth centuries with the new evolutionary psychology and its theories of instinctual behaviours. Despite shifts in theoretical fashion in the intervening period, with a growing recognition of the significance of learning and of culture, the idea of innate or natural sex differences in aggressive behaviour has been enduring.

Instinct theories

As mentioned, the notion of instinct was prominent in early psychology. This has been no less the case in writings about aggression. Instinct theories of aggression have their genesis in the work of writers such as James (1901/1890), a key figure in the development of modern scientific psychology, Thorndike (1921/1913), McDougall (1926/1908) and, most notably, Freud (1930). These writers cannot be said to have articulated a formal theory of aggression and, in fact, the term 'aggression' appears only sporadically in their texts, and then left unexamined. However, they believed that there existed a 'sex instinct' that made men more liable than women to outbursts of 'anger', 'pugnacity', and to 'fighting'. Many descriptions of the period employ a hydraulic metaphor, in analogy to the pressure exercised by dammed-up water or steam in a closed container (Fromm, 1974: 17). Although the hydraulic model of aggression has come to be closely associated with the work of Freud and Lorenz (1966), the idea that 'aggression' is a result of the release of a dammed-up energy has been common among instinct theorists. It can be clearly seen, for instance, in McDougall's discussion of the so-called 'instinct of pugnacity'. According to McDougall, this instinct was unique among the instincts in that it was not stimulated by the perception of any particular object or objects, but rather was excited by opposition to the free reign of other instincts, particularly the male sex instinct (1926: 51–52). The 'hunting instinct' and the 'fighting instinct' were widely seen to be among those frustrated instincts linked to outbursts of 'anger' which, when aroused, were likely to override other instincts such as 'sympathy' and even the 'paternal instinct'. In James' view, these instincts often found an outlet in cruelty towards other animals, in physical attacks on human rivals, in games and sport and in the exercise of property rights. James observed that boys who 'are brought up naturally', take great pleasure in acts of cruelty or acts of destruction of other species of animal, for example by pulling out the wings and legs of flies, by plundering birds' nests, or by tormenting them (James, 1901, footnote: 411–412). Women, he explained, although equally, if not more likely to get angry than men, were seen to be inhibited by 'fear and other principles of their nature from expressing itself in blows'. His view, that 'the hunting instinct proper is decidedly weaker in them than in men', was not uncommon among male psychologists at the time (James, 1901: 415; see also Thorndike, 1921: 84–85).

It would be a mistake to see these early instinct theorists as positing a simple model of biological sex determinism. James, for instance, was aware that there might be some element of learning in the first performance of instinct, and McDougall recognised the moulding influence of different experiences and cultural backgrounds (Fromm, 1974: 13). Drever, who drew extensively on both James' and McDougall's work, was interested in the educational possibilities offered by the psychological study of those instincts seen as most important to human beings and the 'higher animals'; namely, those of the 'emotional type' such as 'fear' and 'anger' (1917: 161–167). Because instincts were seen to constantly threaten to burst forth in destructive ways, it was believed that they needed to be held in check through social institutions, and particularly education. As James explained, instincts needed to be kept under control so that 'the higher powers of mind can be set free for their own proper work' (1901: 122). Thorndike argued that behaviour in all spheres of life (in the family, in business, in the state, in religion, and other spheres) 'is rooted in his ['Man's'] unlearned, original equipment of instincts and capacities'. In his view, psychology could play a key role in studying these instincts so that they could be utilised for the improvement of the individual (Thorndike, 1921: 4). In Thorndike's view, evolutionary psychology had played a role in emphasising 'the selfish and blood-thirsty aggressiveness of our early ancestors and the triumphs of civilization in holding the wild beast within us'. However, it had failed to make clear 'that civilization does not so much create kindness and repress cruelty as merely redirect them' (1921: 105). Like many of his contemporaries, however, Thorndike's reformist vision insofar as women were concerned was limited by what he saw as the generally inferior intellectual capacity of their 'species'. He was one of the foremost exponents of the view, that became an entrenched part of the accepted scientific wisdom about sex differentiation, that male superiority in intellectual and business pursuits could be explained in large measure by greater male variability and female conservatism (Russett, 1989: 99–100).

In Freud's influential work, the dynamics of life and of evolution were explained in terms of the struggle between the instinct of life (preservation) (Eros) and its antithesis, the instinct of destruction or death, which is 'directed towards the outer world' in 'aggressive acts'. The death instinct is 'pressed into the service of Eros' and directed towards some other thing, whether animate or inanimate, because it could end up destroying its own self. Any restriction of this outer-directed 'aggressiveness' is bound to increase self-destruction (1930: 55–56). According to Freud, civilisation is perpetually threatened with disintegration resulting from 'Man's' 'aggressive instincts', which he described as 'the most powerful obstacle to culture', and so must use its utmost efforts to set limits to their expression (1930: 49). For Freud, since civilisation imposes sacrifices on 'Man's' sexuality and 'aggressivity', it is hard for him to be happy, and indeed, he was much happier in his pre-civilised state of being. As Freud explained, 'civilized man has exchanged a portion of happiness for a portion of security' (1930: 52). Freud's model of instinctual behaviour was far more complex than that of other, earlier psychologists, and his 'repression' model acknowledged a dynamic inter-play of instinctual tendencies. Nevertheless, he assumed that men and women were prone to different instinctual imperatives that needed to be held in check through social institutions. In his scheme, men are ascribed the key role in 'the work of civilization' for he believed they are more capable of carrying out instinctual sublimations of which women are incapable.

> Since a man does not have unlimited quantities of psychical energy at his disposal, he has to accomplish his tasks by making an expedient distribution of his libido. What he employs for cultural aims he to a great extent withdraws from women and sexual life. His constant association with men, and his dependence on his relations with them, even estrange him from his duties as a husband and father. Thus the woman finds herself forced into the

background by the claims of civilization and she adopts a hostile attitude towards it. (Freud, 1930: 40–41)

A number of these early instinct theorists proposed the existence of a 'parental instinct' or 'maternal instinct' which, as mentioned, were seen as likely to be overridden by 'the hunting instinct' (e.g. McDougall, 1926: 57–58; Thorndike, 1921: 82–83). Thus, Thorndike observed that 'male thoughtlessness and brutality toward children, and whatever living being or thing makes a similar appeal, is due not to total absence of kindliness, but rather to the presence of the competing tendencies of the hunting instinct'. In his view, this 'is much stronger in men than in women as the maternal instinct is stronger in women than in men' (1921: 84–85). McDougall (1926) noted that the 'parental instinct and the tender emotion' are in the main 'decidedly weaker in men than in women, and in some men, perhaps, altogether lacking'. Although McDougall acknowledged that women were also 'aggressive', this was seen to be linked to the maternal instinct which, when obstructed or opposed, was seen to lead to displays of anger. Thus, 'the least threat, the smallest slight or aspersion (e.g. the mere speaking of the baby as "it", instead of as "he" or "she"), the mere suggestion that it is not the most beautiful object in the world, will suffice to provoke a quick resentment' (1926: 62).

Frustration and aggression

Instinct theories, and Freud's theory of repression in particular, laid the groundwork for a range of new theories of aggression which were based upon implicit or explicit assumptions of 'innate' sex differences. Of particular importance in this regard is the so-called 'frustration–aggression hypothesis', which began to be formulated in the 1930s, and has remained enormously influential in psychology. According to the 'frustration–aggression hypothesis', aggression is a logical and expected product of 'frustration', which is defined as any condition that blocks attainment of a desired goal. Theorists argued that if other conditions prohibit the removal of the 'frustration', 'aggression' may be carried out on other objects (see, e.g. Dollard *et al.*, 1949; Durban and Bowlby, 1939). This theory, which also employs a hydraulic metaphor, has proved to be highly controversial because of the assumption that each and every aggressive response ultimately derives from a frustrating experience (Zillman, 1984: 9). Explanations of sex-linked aggression assume the existence of a natural male sexual drive that seeks release. In the context of frustration–aggression theory, 'sexual frustration' is just another form of frustration. Thus, male violence against women and children has been ascribed to sexual frustration. But some proponents of this theory have gone so far as to argue that curtailing sexual behaviour is responsible not just for the behaviour of some individuals who are excessively violent, but for high levels of aggressiveness in entire cultures. Sexual violence is assumed to be a more or less exclusively male behaviour, and in some accounts is seen to derive from non-sexual frustrations (e.g. failure in professional endeavours) as much as from sexual ones (Zillman, 1984: 9–10). The assumption of natural sex differences in aggression is apparent in the choice of supportive evidence, such as that deriving from studies of fighting behaviour resulting from 'sexual rivalry', particularly among monkeys and apes and 'some of the simplest peoples [who] live in societies identical in structure to those of baboons' (see Durban and Bowlby, 1939: 59). Durban and Bowlby turned to such evidence for casting light on the origins of war. After reviewing the findings of observational studies of fighting among colonies of monkeys and apes, and anthropological studies of sexual rivalry among the 'simplest peoples' such as Australian 'natives', the Chinook Indians, and Greenlanders, they concluded that 'although there may be various causes of fighting, it appears that, as in baboons, one of its principle sources is over the possession of wives' (1939: 62).

The assumption of natural sex differences is also evident in Erich Fromm's Freudo-Marxian version of the 'frustration–aggression' theory. It is implicit in the evolutionary theory which he draws upon in his analysis, and which he fails to critically interrogate, and in his assumption about the 'naturalness' of the sex/gender system. His work reflects a masculine gender bias in his repeated use of the generic term 'Man'. For instance, Fromm draws a distinction between 'defensive aggression' (or 'benign aggression') which is biologically adaptive for both animals and 'Man', and the specifically human 'malignant aggression', which 'does not serve the physiological survival of man, yet...is an important part of his mental functioning'. According to Fromm, the former kind of aggression is a 'fight or flight' reaction when 'vital interests are threatened', but is seen to be potentially more explosive in humans, partly because of the more complex neurophysiology of the human brain. It is also due to the 'specific conditions of *human* existence': the 'capacity for foresight and imagination', the potential for 'Man' to be 'persuaded and brainwashed by his leaders to see dangers when in reality they do not exist', and a much greater range of vital interests to be protected than that of the animal (1974: 195–197; emphasis in original). 'Malignant aggression', on the other hand, Fromm argues, is a destructive, cruel aggression which 'is one of the possible answers to psychic needs that are rooted in the existence of man', and results from '*the interaction of various social conditions with man's existential needs*' (1974: 218; emphases in original). In Fromm's analysis, 'aggression' is coded masculine and is a product of frustration of socially generated psychic needs such as the need for love, which results in the development of a negative passion: absolute control of life or destruction. (Fromm's ideas on aggression, specifically as they relate to war, are discussed further in Chapter 3.)

The influence of hormones and chromosomes

The idea of innate sex difference in aggressivity has also found expression in theories of chromosome and hormone-based behaviours which began to gain increasing popularity from the 1920s onwards (Bullough, 1994: 122–132, 213–215; Oudshoorn, 1994; Van den Wijngaard, 1991). The development of hormone studies and human genetics were major factors in launching gender studies, and have continued to generate controversy and research on sex differences, including research on sex-linked aggression. The 'discovery' of chromosomes eventually led to research that linked excessive male aggression and violence with the existence of an extra Y chromosome (i.e. an XYY karyotype). It has been suggested by some researchers that since Y is the chromosome of aggression, doubling Y doubles aggression (Lissey *et al.*, 1973). Support for the argument of extreme aggression in the XYY karyotype is made on the grounds that the anomaly is more frequently found in institutions for the criminally insane and that proportions are even higher in maximum security prisons (see Court-Brown, 1967; Jacobs *et al.*, 1965; Zillman, 1984: 100). This theory can be seen to have its antecedents in nineteenth century theories of the physiognomists such as Lombroso who identified the born criminal as a distinctive anthropological type (Lombroso, 1911). It has since been discredited by most psychologists, especially following the publication in 1976 of an extensive study of convicted XYYs which found no evidence that this group is more likely to commit crimes of violence than XYs (Witkin *et al.*, 1976). Another perspective on this difference discourse, which begins with the acknowledgement that females, too, can be aggressive, is that the X chromosome *inhibits* aggression, and that females have a greater aggression inhibition because they have a second X chromosome (Josephson and Colwill, 1978: 204).

In hormonal theory, it is testosterone that is seen to explain the more aggressive behaviour of males. According to researchers, hormones affect human conduct by either (i) organising the developing human brain in such a way that particular modes of response become more likely; or (ii) by activating the physiological mechanisms that help to govern certain behavioural patterns. In the former case, 'a relatively high concentration of testosterone can push its [the growing fetus'] central nervous system in a masculine direction', causing it to develop 'masculine physical characteristics' and 'malelike' behaviours (Berkowitz, 1993: 397). Although researchers acknowledge that evidence for the latter proposition is not entirely clear since, 'for ethical reasons, it isn't possible to do the kind of experiment that would be required to establish such proof', there is a tradition of research establishing links between high levels of testosterone and male 'anti-social conduct' (e.g. prison inmates with histories of violent crimes) and self-reports of physically or verbally aggressive response (Berkowitz, 1993: 398–399). Abnormal levels of testosterone, which lead to aggression, are also seen to be possibly explained, in some cases, by the XYY syndrome (see Wiggings *et al.*, 1971, cited in Josephson and Colwill, 1978: 203). The hormonal theorists of aggression often argue their case by referring to animal (generally mice or chimpanzees) studies that show that, first, castrated males, when given the opportunity to fight, 'behave like females' in that they remain peaceful, and secondly, when these animals are given doses of male hormone, they immediately start fighting (see, e.g. Scott, 1958: 71). There have been a number of detailed feminist analyses of hormonal explanations of aggression, especially those based on animal studies. Among the criticisms made include the charge that animal research is anthropomorphic, that writings confuse or interchange social and biological concepts, and that the findings of such research are used to legitimate the unequal treatment of women (see Bleier, 1984: 80–114; Fausto-Stirling, 1992:

123–154). However, this theory continues to enjoy widespread popularity among some scientists and members of the broader public and has often been invoked in calls for the castration of rapists and other sex offenders as a solution to sexual violence against women and children (Fausto-Sterling, 1992: 126).

Innate sex differences in preparedness to learn

The idea that men and women are differently equipped in *preparedness to learn* aggressive responses became increasingly popular with the emergence of social learning theory in the 1940s and 1950s. Social learning theory became popular in a context of concerns about resurgent eugenics in the aftermath of the Nazi period and widespread aversion to overt theories of biological difference. The theory states that children learn behaviours through observing their parents. They learn behaviours without any direct reinforcement because they see their parents as powerful, and as having control over rewards. However, when the children come to perform the behaviours they have learned, they are differentially reinforced (Kessler and McKenna, 1985: 92). There are numerous versions of learning theory. One version postulates that females are disadvantaged in size and strength, and so any physical aggression in which they do engage is less likely to meet with the reinforcement of success. Frodi *et al.* (1977) have proposed that males and females exhibit differences in 'aggression anxiety' as measured by reported levels of guilt and anxiety about aggressing. In the influential work of Albert Bandura, sex differences in aggression result from a combination of observation, imitation, indoctrination, and conscious learning. Sex-appropriate behaviours are learnt through the administering of punishments and rewards (Bandura, 1977; Bandura and Walters, 1963). For example, parents may reinforce the assertive behaviour of the young boy by attending to their 'demands' (e.g. crying), but ignore a similar behaviour in the daughter. Some behaviourists have argued that the two sexes are reinforced for different forms of aggression. Thus, girls are allowed to show hostility in subtle ('catty') ways, but not physical ways. Whereas physical aggression is thought appropriate for boys, 'cattiness' is not (Maccoby and Jacklin, 1974: 229–234). The assumption that adults reinforce boys' aggression more than girls' aggression, and that behaviour is more often reinforced when children imitate a same-sex rather than an opposite-sex model, has been questioned by Maccoby and Jacklin (1974), in their extensive review of the literature of the psychology of sex differences. However, even they accept the premise that the learning of sex-typed behaviour is 'a process built upon biological foundations that are sex-differentiated to some degree' (1974: 363–364).

Learning theory has provided the underpinning for a proliferation of writings on the relationship between the 'male sex role' and 'aggression'. From the perspective of role theory, the male learns aggression as a script. They learn this script through observing and imitating the skilled performance of other dominant male figures, particularly fathers. Unfortunately, so argue the theory's proponents, this is a performance that constrains the performer, and oppresses other actors (especially women), and should therefore be unlearned. David and Brannon (1976), for example, in their book *The Forty-Nine Percent Majority*, argue that feminism brought to light the constraints of the 'cultural blueprint' that is the 'female sex role', but had bypassed consideration of the distinctly male blueprint that is the 'male sex role'. As they explain, the male sex role is one that entails 'aggressiveness', an attribute which is seen as 'natural and normal' in business and academic life, in sport and popular culture, in sexual encounters, and in other contexts (1976: 27–35). According to its proponents, the social role explanation of sex differences in aggression admits the possibility of social change. If gender roles are imposed on individuals by society then there exists the potential for them to be removed (see, e.g. Lightdale and Prentice, 1994).

How exactly does the male become aggressive according to sex role theory? In an influential version of the theory, the Male Sex Role Identity Paradigm (MSRI) of Pleck (*The Myth of Masculinity* (1981)) the individual is 'pre-programmed' to develop sex role identity as part of 'normal' psychological development. There is, in other words, an innate predisposition to seek an appropriate role identity which, for men, includes expressions of aggressive behaviour. Thus, culturally defined sex roles do not arbitrarily restrict the individual's potential, but are 'necessary external structures without which individuals could not develop normally'. In this view, the nature of roles themselves is not a problem, but rather that 'so many people fail to fit them' (Pleck, 1981: 4). The development of an appropriate sex role identity is for males a particularly 'risky, failure-prone process', and homosexuality is a clear indication of 'a disturbance of sex role identity' (1981: 4).

Aggression and violence are seen to be a result of male insecurity in sex role identity, resulting in particular from 'maternal domination' (1981: 96–115). The idea that problems in sex role identity result from 'maternal domination' or the absence of a male is a common theme in sex role theory. It takes monogamous heterosexuality as the norm and it invariably traces the origins of all pathology back to the mother who is seen to fail to meet the male child's needs. In the psychoanalytic work of Rochlin, *Man's Aggression: The Defence of the Self* (1973) and *The Masculine Dilemma: A Psychology of Masculinity* (1980), violence or forms of aggression are seen to be 'narcissistic reactions associated with threatened masculinity' resulting from recurrent fears and wishes to be feminine. For a boy, the identification with the mother never loses significance in relation to his becoming masculine and it gives rise to lasting complex reactions and defences (1980: 10). This is the classic male Oedipal crisis described by Freud: the male develops a strong emotional attachment to his mother but comes to fear his father's retaliation for his attachment and, in particular, fears that he will be castrated (literally or symbolically), and deals with this fear by becoming like his father and rejecting his mother. Masculinity is a perilous performance, and identifying oneself with the aggressor (i.e. the father) offers the surest form of defence against loss of (male) identity.

In short, while learning theory would seem to offer a challenge to earlier theories about the innate character of sex or gender differences in aggression it, too, is underpinned by assumptions about natural differences in development. These assumptions are imported via theories that postulate natural differences in propensity to learn, which are then reinforced through social conditioning, or via the psychoanalytic framework used to explain sex role socialisation. As I have explained, the notion that there is an 'essential' difference between men and women, which is founded on biology, and that this difference is adaptive for the species and functional for the individual and society, reflects the enduring and pervasive influence of Darwinian thinking and complementary theories. These ideas, I would argue, continue to hold sway in academic writings as well as in popular discourse – on which more will be said later. However, before doing so, so as not to leave the discussion incomplete, I should first offer some assessment of an approach that has had growing influence in psychology in general, and the psychology of gender and emotion in particular, in recent years, namely social constructionism.

Psychology and socially constructionism

As noted in Chapter 1, the social constructionist approach has recently found some adherents in psychology (e.g. Fischer, 2000; Harré, 1986; Harré and Parrott, 1996). This would seem to offer a radical challenge to the discipline's established 'ways of knowing'. Writing in the mid-1980s, in his book *The Social Construction of Emotions*, Rom Harré noted that 'the overwhelming evidence of cultural diversity and cognitive differentiation in the emotions of mankind has become so obvious that a new consensus is developing around the idea of social construction' (1986: 3). As noted in Chapter 1, constructionism encompasses a range of approaches, but social constructionists tend to share a view on the relativity of knowledge and acknowledge that that which is socially constructed is not inevitable. According to Gergen, 'social constructionist theory is an approach to understanding forms of knowledge that emphasises the significance of language communities in creating and sustaining our sense of reality' (Gergen, 2001). In Burr's view, a social constructionist approach tends to include one or more of the following assumptions. These are: a critical stance towards taken-for-granted knowledge; acknowledgement that the categories and concepts we use for understanding our world are historically and culturally specific; recognition that knowledge is sustained by social processes, and that knowledge and social action are inter-linked (Burr, 1995: 2–5).

Harré himself proposed that social constructionism would ask how particular emotion terms, such as 'anger', are actually used in certain cultural milieu and type of episode. He believed that uncovering the basis of usage would bring the psychology of emotions a degree of sophistication that it sadly lacked (Harré, 1986: 5). As he explained,

The first step to a more sophisticated theory will be to show how, in the research, priority must be given to obtaining a proper understanding of how various emotion vocabularies are used. Recent work . . . has shown that the very idea of an emotion as a response suffered by a passive participant in some emotive event is itself part of the social strategies by which emotions and emotion declarations are used by people in certain interactions. This is not to deny that there are 'leakages' into consciousness from raised heartbeat, increased sweating, swollen tear ducts and so on. But these effects are incidental to what it is to be in this or that emotional state. It turns out that the dominant contribution to the way that aspect of our lives unfolds comes from the local social world, by way of its linguistic practices and the moral judgements in the course of which the emotional quality of encounters is defined. Turning our attention away from the physiological states of individuals to the unfolding of social practices opens up the possibility that many emotions can exist only in the reciprocal exchanges of a social encounter. (Harré, 1986: 5)

On the face of it, this focus on linguistic practices and the social context offers a radical challenge to conventional psychological understandings of gender and emotion strongly based as they have been on biological categories. What counts as 'reality' is relative to time, place, and particular language communities and hence is subject to challenge and change. The concept of the natural, and the category of 'biology', are 'constructed' or 'made' – that is, products of culture – and hence can be 'de-constructed' or 're-made' (see, e.g. Shilling, 1993: Chapter 4; Yanagisako and Delaney, 1995). Differences, such as those between 'male' and 'female' are not natural differences but rather are made to appear as the logical outgrowths of other 'facts of life' (Yanagisako and Delaney, 1995: 11). When one closely examines how psychologists' deploy social constructionism in their work, however, it is often not clear what is critical or radically different about their approach to knowledge.

A major difficulty arises from lack of clarity in definitions. In studies, the term 'social construction' is often left undefined, or is defined loosely. In his book *The Social Construction of What?* (1999), Ian Hacking has drawn attention to the overuse and imprecise use of the term 'social construction' and the failure of writers to acknowledge the premises and biases which underlie particular versions of social constructionism. As Hacking points out, when writers refer to 'The social construction of x', what they mean, or seem to mean, is the construction of *the idea* of x, the classification or the kind of person that is the subject of analysis. The implication of employing the metaphor of construction is that x need not have existed and is not universal (Hacking, 1999: 10–19). At first glance, this appears a radical proposition, which clearly has political implications. In some 'schools' of social constructionism, especially those influenced by the work of Michel Foucault, the political strategy lies in 'making strange' through a particular form of historical investigation, the naturalness or self-evident character of the present; for example psychology's concepts of 'the child', 'boys' and 'girls' (Tyler, 1997: 78–80). However, as it has been applied to the analysis of emotions, Hacking argues, the word 'construct' has lost all its force. That is, when people say that emotion is socially constructed they do not mean that the idea of the emotions is constructed, but that the emotions themselves are social constructs (Hacking, 1999: 18). Psychologists who have been influenced by social constructionism often refer to evidence showing that the categories of emotion and hence emotional experience and expression vary from culture to culture, which challenges traditional approaches which focus on the universality of emotion as measured, for example, by facial expressions (see, e.g. Wierzbicka, 1999). However, as Hacking argues, the validity of this argument hinges on the author's definition of emotions. In his view, in such discussions, the label 'social construction' is 'more code than description': that is, it is code for not universal, offering a corrective to the tendency to invoke a 'pan-cultural human nature' (Hacking, 1999: 19). He concurs with Griffiths (1997), who argues that the insights of social constructionism as applied to the emotions are not necessarily incompatible with the evolutionary perspective on emotion (Hacking, 1999: 19). Since the discussion is not about something that is literally constructed, Hacking argues, it is not clear that it is useful to use construction talk at all (1999: 19).

In many psychological works based on a social constructionist approach to emotions there is an evident tension between the search for universal aspects of emotional experience and recognition of the need to acknowledge culturally specific aspects of experience. For some writers, social constructionism is taken to mean that emotions are *products* of culture rather than simply being influenced by culture (e.g. Cornelius, 1996: 150). For others, however, it means that 'distinct cultural patterns of emotions emerge from a limited range of universal emotions' (Madden *et al.*, 2000: 289). In psychological studies of emotion, language and beliefs are often taken as surrogates for 'culture' which are seen to shape the categories or definitions of emotion and the experience and expression of emotion. Analyses of sex/gender differences in emotion often focus on differences in language use and styles of emotional expression; for example, facial gestures. Scholars have observed that 'emotion vocabularies' vary across cultures (Fischer, 1995). Some writers speak of culturally specific 'emotional display rules': different cultures have different expectations about the most appropriate way to express emotion (e.g. Western, 1999: 489) (see Chapter 5). It is argued that such display rules differ not only by culture but also by gender. Thus, Western suggests, on the basis of 'best evidence', that 'women probably experience emotion more intensely, are better able to read emotions from other people's faces and nonverbal cues, and express emotion more intensely and openly than men' (Western 1999, citing Brody and Hall, 1993). In effect, this is a reworking and updating of social learning theory which, as mentioned, began to emerge in the 1940s and 1950s during a period when there was widespread aversion to overt theories of biological difference. That is, by learning the culturally prescribed 'feeling rules' for those of their gender, men and women are socialised into different emotional worlds. 'Stereotypes' are seen to provide the basis for socialising girls and boys about appropriate emotional behaviour and thus differences in reinforcement histories lead to differences in expressions of emotion such as sadness and fear. Girls are socialised to express fear and sadness, whereas boys are not (Madden *et al.*, 2000: 279).

One way in which social constructionist approaches differ from earlier learning theories is in acknowledging that 'culture' varies, and hence that men and women can learn their emotional roles in different ways. However, this does not necessarily mean the denial of 'emotional universals' – indeed cross-cultural work has been undertaken by researchers of emotion in order to identify 'true universals' and to debunk 'false universals' which are seen to arise from ethnocentrism (see, e.g. Wierzbicka, 1999: Chapter 7). In some recent work, there is acknowledgement of the power relations associated with sex differences in socialisation (e.g. Brody and Hall, 1993; Fischer, 1995; Shields, 2000). For example, the emotions that women display more (e.g. warmth, happiness, shame, guilt, fear, and nervousness) are seen as consistent with women's lower social status and power, and traditional gender roles (Brody and Hall, 1993: 452). Men and women are seen to have different entitlements in exercising rights to emotion and different opportunities to exercise power through displays of emotion; for example, anger (Shields, 2000: 16–17; see also Fischer, 1995: 459–462). However, despite the introduction of a political dimension to some of this work, there has been a lack of reflection on how psychology *through the study of sex/gender and emotion* 'makes up' the categories 'men' and 'women' as different. There has been little research into how psychology shapes knowledge of men's and women's emotionality through the questions pursued, the particular methods adopted in studies, and the categories and concepts used in analysis. As in other fields of psychological study, psychologists of sex/gender and emotion have, in the main, been blind to questions of history and to the fact that their 'ways of knowing' are historically contingent and closely linked with prevailing modes or rule (see, e.g. Rose, 1989, 1996).

Conclusion

During its history, psychology has developed many theories to account for apparent differences between men and women. However, despite shifts in theoretical focus and varying emphases on 'nature' and 'culture', psychology has had an enduring concern with the innate basis of difference, reflecting the profound influence of the evolutionary theories of Darwin. Darwin's ideas have continued to inspire, particularly in evolutionary psychology, a field of study that explains an array of mental attributes, behaviours, and dispositions. The recent emergence of social constructionism would seem to offer a radical challenge to psychology's 'ways of knowing', including the study of gender differences in aggression. However, as noted, the term 'social construction' suffers from overuse and a lack of clarity in definition. Constructionist studies are critical of basic categories and concepts to varying degrees. While some social constructionist work has a strong political dimension, on the whole, relatively little attention has been paid to the construction and politics of psychological knowledge itself. Psychology contributes to the production of knowledge about difference that is promulgated through various means, including education and training and advice literature. In the following chapters, I focus on a number of contexts where such theories find extensive application, namely the military and war, and love, intimacy, and sex.

3
Gender, Emotion, and War

The close links between definitions of gender and emotion is perhaps nowhere more evident than in the institutions of the military and in the theatres of war. Ongoing debates about women's involvement in combat roles and popular cultural depictions of the male warrior in warfare rely upon generalised views of men's and women's emotional make-up. Military institutions provide the means for disciplining bodies and shaping minds, and categorising and separating the 'fit' and the 'unfit'. The bastardisation rituals of the military, vividly portrayed in the film *Full Metal Jacket* (1987), aim to re-socialise individuals, by stripping them of civilian identities and establishing new soldier identities: emotionally distanced killing machines. War provides the occasion for demonstrating the virtues of 'manliness' and essential differences between men and women. News media and other popular cultural portrayals of war are heavily masculinised. They reinforce the view that war is essentially 'men's business', that war is an expression of an innate male aggressivity, and that men are natural protectors and women the protected. Many people's experiences of war, particularly in the Western world, is via the media rather than through direct experience, a point increasingly recognised by political authorities, who have sought to control the media and its images in the 'battle for hearts'. The media has become a crucial site for contests over portrayals and definitions of truth and is thus an intrinsic part of the machinery of war.

This chapter explores the significance of the military and warfare as contexts for engendering emotions. Focusing on some influential and recent texts on the origins of warfare, it begins by examining some enduring beliefs about the links between aggression, gender, and war. These beliefs contribute to the public discourse about war, and its gender-related emotional origins and impacts. It then goes on to examine the role of language, visual images of news media, and the practices of war in defining differences and governing relations between the sexes. Theories of psychology, biology, and other sciences have been used extensively in warfare, in the training of soldiers, in explaining the origins of war, and in justifying the fact of war and the many atrocities (e.g. rape) committed during the course of battle. In the following paragraphs, I will show how some of these theories have been applied in the training and disciplining of soldiers and in making up 'men' and 'women' as different. In explanations of warfare, there is a long history of arguments about men's innate aggressive natures, or 'society's need' for an outlet for collective sentiment of 'guilt' or pent-up tension. Scientific knowledge has been applied in the effort to harness and channel these energies for particular political purposes and to legitimate military decisions that have been made. The chapter explores some specific instances where such ideas have been deployed and the means by which they are propagated. It concludes by examining the implications of the changing technologies, contexts, and meanings of war (particularly the increasing focus on 'terrorism') for gender–emotion associations.

Enduring beliefs about gender, aggression and war

In the long tradition of theorising about the origins of warfare there have been a number of recurring ideas and arguments about the connections between gender, aggression and war. Contributions have been diverse, but are much indebted to the biological and psychological theories of the nineteenth and early twentieth centuries, and particularly to the contributions of Charles Darwin and Sigmund Freud. The view that war is the result of an 'innate' or 'instinctual' aggression in 'man' and is therefore inevitable has been a dominant theme in the literature. Although accounts of the origins of warfare do not always make explicit reference to the influence of sex/gender, in writings, 'aggression' is generally coded masculine and the aggressive instinct that is referred to is generally assumed to be the *male* aggressive instinct. A number of dualisms underlie views about gender differences in aggression and in the capacity to fight: nature/nurture, protector/

protected, active/passive, rational/emotive, good/evil, death/life, combatant/non-combatant, front/homefront, and controlled/disruptive. A common argument is that 'men' are genetically 'programmed' for aggression and that consequently fighting wars is 'natural' and inevitable (Rosoff, 1991). Women, on the other hand, are seen as lacking the 'killer instinct' and hence as being unsuited to combat roles. Evolutionary psychology, which draws extensively on evidence from the animal kingdom (see Chapter 2), has in particular lent support to the view that warfare is a result of 'hard-wired', genetically determined (male) impulses and is thus largely unavoidable. The limitations of drawing inferences about human behaviour from animal behaviour (anthropomorphising) are now well understood (see, e.g. Goldstein, 1989; Huntingford, 1989). Even if one accepted that one could draw meaningful analogies from the animal behaviour, and somehow separate out the values and assumptions of researchers, there remains the question of how to define 'aggression'. As indicated in Chapter 2, scholars often use 'aggression' in an uncritical way, as though its meaning is self-evident, whereas its definitions vary across cultures and through time. Further, some writers have equated 'aggression' – an individual level phenomenon – with 'warfare' – a group level phenomenon. Definitions of 'war' are also notoriously difficult, and increasingly so with the erosion of hegemonic discourse and the challenge to the binaries that war had originally inspired (Cooke, 1993: 182). Notwithstanding definitional problems, the language of war often has positive connotations, as seen in its applications in business and athletic contexts, 'to emphasize dedicated struggle to forward a large cause'; for example the 'war on drugs, poverty, disease and crime' (De Pauw, 1998: 11).

The ideas of Sigmund Freud have been highly influential in writings about the instinctual origins of aggression and war. However, additional influences include the researches of some ethologists and sociobiologists (e.g. Konrad Lorenz, 1966); research on the brain; theories of genetic determination; and the biological emphasis in the mass media's portrayal of violence and aggression research (Goldstein, 1989: 12). As argued in Chapter 2, Freud posited a complex view of the instinctual basis of aggressive behaviour, which needed to be kept under control by civilisation. Though constrained by the concepts and terminology of his own time, his work revealed a more sophisticated understanding of the motivations for human action than that held by other instinctivists (Fromm, 1974: 14–20, 439–478). In particular, Freud acknowledged the influence of the environment (essentially the significant persons in early childhood) and the unconscious desires that are repressed for the sake of self-preservation. Freud's view on war can be explained in terms of the resolution of the tension between the two opposing life forces, the 'death instinct' and the 'life instinct' or the instinct of preservation. The former instinct, he argued, is either directed towards the organism itself, and is thus self-destructive, or is directed outwards, in which case it tends to destroy others rather than oneself (see Chapter 2). Suppressing aggression was in general unhealthy and leads to illness. For 'Man', then, the tragic dilemma is either to suppress aggression and become sick or to wage war, to be aggressive, to avoid sickness. Here, as in other writings of the period, one can see evidence of the hydraulic metaphor: the notion that aggression is like an explosive energy that is bottled up and demands release in action and expression at frequent intervals (Solomon, 1993: 77–82). For Freud, war would seem to be an inevitable outcome of the effort to maintain the health and continuity of the species, and is subject to little modification by the environment.

As indicated earlier, Freud's work has been criticised by feminist scholars for, among other things, its masculine bias and its implicit heterosexism (Rowley and Grosz, 1990). As Fromm himself commented, 'Freud was deeply imbued with the patriarchal feeling that men were superior to women, and not their equals', a male bias that 'had, at a much earlier period, led him to the theory that women were crippled men, governed by the castration complex and penis envy, inferior to men also by the fact that their superego is weaker, their narcissism, however, stronger than that of men' (Fromm, 1974: 459–460). The assumed human subject of Freud's theory of aggression is masculine, a bias which has subsequently continued in the contributions of many others. Under the influence of Freud, a number of writers have subsequently proposed that war stems from 'Man's' underlying psychic needs, which find expression in the collective fantasies and actions of whole nations of peoples.

Fromm, whose contributions to the psychology of aggression were referred to earlier, also drew on psychoanalytic theory, as well as other fields of study, to present a sophisticated account of aggression and war. As noted in Chapter 2, Fromm believed that there are two basic kinds of aggression, each of which has different sources and qualities: 'defensive' or 'benign' aggression that serves the survival of the individual and the species, and is biologically adaptive, and 'malignant' aggression, which is cruel and destructive, and is specific to the human species. War, Fromm argues, is a benign form of aggression, what he calls 'instrumental aggression', in that its aim is not destruction per se, but rather obtaining that that is necessary or desirable. In other words, he rejects the notion, subscribed to by many instinctivists and psychoanalysts, that humans have an innate tendency for war. According to Fromm, the claim that war is caused by an innate tendency is repudiated by the historical record and by the history of primitive warfare, which shows that 'the hunters and food gatherers ... are the least warlike, and [that] their fighting is characterized by its relative lack of destructiveness and bloodthirstiness.' He believed that war is likely to be motivated by a range of factors including, economic interests, and political, military, and industrial ambitions. For example, the German's aims in the 1914–18 war were 'economic hegemony in Western and Central Europe and the territory in the East' – aims that were also shared by Hitler and by the Western allies (Fromm, 1974: 212). However, once war has commenced, 'deep-seated human impulses, such as altruism and solidarity', which in times of peace are 'stunted', are encouraged, providing the motivation to continue fighting (Fromm, 1974: 214). Fromm argued that, although it is not possible to change the biological basis of defensive aggression, it can be controlled and modified, particularly through changing those conditions which mobilise aggression, especially threats by others. In his view, the development of a war-free society required a different system production, ownership, and consumption – one that provided the basic necessities for all. This would involve 'radical and political changes that would alter all human relations, including the family structure, the structure of education, of religion, and relations between individuals in work and leisure' (Fromm, 1974: 216–217).

A recent psychoanalytic contribution to thinking about the origins of war is deMause's *The Emotional Life of Nations* (2002). In this 'psychohistorical' account, deMause argues that war and violence have their origins in the fantasies of whole nations, particularly the desire to 'cleanse' the 'inner pollution' of sin and guilt arising from extended periods of prosperity. Different child-rearing practices, deMause contends, can help explain different individual and national propensities to undertake wars and to kill others. As in many other psychoanalytic writings, no explicit theory of sex or gender differences is offered. However, leaders such as Ronald Reagan, George Bush Senior, and Sadam Hussein, who all happen to be male, are cited as having been unable to resist their nations' call to war because they were abused as children. Writing in the shadow of the events of September 11, 2001 (the attack on the World Trade Centre in New York), deMause traces the roots of 'current terrorist attacks' 'not to this or that American foreign policy error but in the extremely abusive families of the terrorists' (deMause, 2002: 39). As deMause explains, the abuse of children, including the genital mutilation of girls, in fundamentalist families, is at the basis of Islamic terrorism. Wife beating, rape, and the denial of pleasure in general are presented as endemic to fundamentalist Islamic cultures and as explaining violence.

> From childhood . . . Islamic terrorists have been taught to kill the part of themselves – and, by projection, others – that is selfish and wants personal pleasures and freedoms. It is in the terror-filled homes – not just later in the terrorist training camps – that they first learn to be martyrs and to die for Allah . . . Like serial killers – who are also sexually and physically abused as children – terrorists grow up filled with rage that must be inflicted upon others . . . (de Mause, 2002: 44–45)

What deMause fails to explain is the gendered nature of 'terrorist' violence, with men rather than women being the chief perpetrators. If a violent childhood is the key to violence by adults in fundamentalist Islamic cultures, why are not women, who are very often the main victims of violence, the chief perpetrators? Further, deMause overlooks the specific socio-economic, cultural, religious, and other factors that give rise to the phenomenon of terrorism and fails to explain why 'Islamic terrorists' have directed their violence at particular targets. The US involvement in war, deMause observes, has followed long periods of peace and prosperity. The US decided to go to war in the Persian Gulf in 1991 for 'strong irrational reasons' – to solve the nation's prosperity-induced emotional problems – rather than for economic or other reasons. In the case of the US aggression abroad, the enemy is created and often armed, as in the case of Sadam Hussein's regime in Iraq, and then blamed for the country's 'greediness' and then punished instead of punishing itself (deMause, 2002: 19–20). De Mause's emphasis on the 'psychogenetic sources of war' leads him to ignore the significance of international forces and gender relations of power in the origins of war and violence. Attention is focused narrowly on individual and biological explanations and implications (see deMause, 2002: 142–181) to the neglect of social, economic and political sources and solutions.

Darwin's influence on writings about aggression and war is especially evident in sociobiology, which emerged in the 1970s. According to sociobiologists, aggression and warfare are adaptive, that is, they have evolved in response to competition for a common resource or requirement. In the view of Edward Wilson, sexual competition and resource competition are especially significant triggers for aggressive behaviour and for the 'violent machismo of males' (Wilson, 1975: 243). The idea that sexual competition lies at the basis of aggression and warfare can be traced directly back to Darwin. In his studies of mammals, Darwin noted that if males rather than females had 'weapons' (e.g. horns of a larger size) then these must be for intramale competition which had been gained through a process of sexual selection whereby the stronger defeated the weaker (Darwin, 1872). Although Wilson acknowledged the role that learning plays in shaping aggressive behaviours, this itself is seen as ultimately under the control of genetic factors. Wilson asks, 'Is aggression in man adaptive?', to which he responds:

> From the biologists point of view it certainly seems to be. It is hard to believe that any characteristic so widespread and easily provoked in a species as aggressive behaviour in man could be neutral or negative in its effects on individual survival and reproduction. To be sure, overt aggressiveness is not a trait in all or even a majority of human cultures. But in order to be adaptive it is enough that aggressive patterns be evoked only under certain conditions of stress such as those that might arise during food shortages and periodic high population densities. It also does not matter whether aggression is wholly innate or is acquired part or wholly by learning. We are now sophisticated enough to know that the capacity to learn certain behaviours is itself a genetically controlled and therefore evolved trait. (Wilson, 1975: 254–255)

In Wilson's view, aggressive behaviour, like ethics, religion, and a whole range of other human institutions and behaviours 'evolve so as to further the welfare of their practitioners' (Wilson, 1975: 561). Virtually any institution or practice, including warfare, that is enduring can be explained in terms of its adaptive value; that is, the benefits it confers for the survival of the group or species. Like other socio-biologists and evolutionary psychologists of a later period, Wilson relies heavily on the study of other animal species to support his arguments about the innate character of human aggression. The animal world and the human world are viewed as mirrors of the other. Anthropomorphism is evident in Wilson's description of 'warfare' and 'aggressive' behaviours among ant colonies and other animals (Wilson, 1975: 244). Again, as with the psychoanalytic theorists, issues of power relations and sex/gender difference are ignored. Aggression, violence, and war are seen as 'facts of life', as products of 'man's' biological evolution, and hence inevitable. Sex/ gender differences and relations are taken as given, and hence assumed to be adaptive and functional for the species.

In the above body of work one can see the considerable influence of theories of evolutionary biology on thinking about the origins of war and about sex/gender differences in aggression and propensity to participate in war. Relatively few writers have questioned the fact of differences between men and women in their potential for 'aggression' or participation in warfare, or sought to investigate how the categories of emotion are mobilised and utilised in the contexts of the military and war for the engendering of persons. The significance of particular gender–emotion associations for specific political objectives and practices is left largely unexplored. Theweleit's (1987, 1989) psycho-analytic analysis of the Freidkorps in pre-world war two Germany is one of the few exceptions. Power relations, and particularly the power relations of gender, are central to Theweleit's *Male Fantasies* (1987/1989), which presents a psychoanalytic account of the emotional underpinnings of fascist militarism. Focusing on the period 1918 to 1928, when the German Freikorps emerged, Theweleit explores the formation of a political culture out of which Nazism eventually developed. According to Theweleit, the male self is in constant danger of disintegration and therefore needs to be differentiated from 'the other', particularly the feminine, which is subverted. The flight from the feminine represents a fear of ego dissolution and warfare is 'the fulfilment of a longing for fusion (with the military machine) and legitimate explosion in the moment of battle' (Benjamin and Rabinbach, 1989: xvii). He describes the physical and mental training undertaken by the German fascist recruit to forge a male self and the hate expressed by Freikorpsmen towards women, specifically women's bodies and sexuality. In Theweleit's view, fascism is not just of historical interest but is already implicit in the daily relationships of men and women. The enactment of war is integral to the reproduction of the division between the genders. The male soldier's commitment and sense of duty to the 'larger whole' expresses an ever-present fear of the fragmentation and dissolution of the self. In training his body to be hard, impenetrable and machine-like, the soldier learns to exclude that which is soft, feminine, and fluid. The military academy serves to 'reconstruct' male bodies, making them obedient to a father figure (the Führer) and placing them in a hierarchical relationship to each other and to fear 'other' bodies, particularly those of women and homosexuals (Theweleit, 1989: Chapter 2). As Theweleit's work makes clear, ideas about gender differences in emotion are (re)produced via a variety of mechanisms and media in the contexts of military and warfare: in news and other popular media portrayals of battles, through practices of employment and deployment (e.g. in combat roles), via the routines of training, and in military language. In the following paragraphs, I examine some of these mechanisms and media, beginning with the illustrative example of news reporting of the Gulf War in 2003.

The role of the news media: the case of the 2003 Gulf War

The news media is a powerful source for images of the links between gender, emotion, and war. For many people in the contemporary Western world, their only experience of war is via television and newspapers. That war is a mass-mediated and 'staged' event was demonstrated by the Gulf Wars of 1990–91 and 2003 (see, e.g. Baudrillard, 1995). During those wars, the military was able to exert considerable control over the news portrayal of events. Recent research on the role of the media in war highlights the close interdependence between the institutions of the military and the institutions of the media that undermines the notion of an independent and critical media. This work has identified many organisational and ideological constraints that prevent the media from presenting conflicts in an unbiased manner (see, e.g. Thussu and Freedman, 2003). Although journalistic practice continues to be guided by the ideals of 'independence' and 'objectivity', a number of macro forces, including globalisation, concentration of media ownership, increased competitiveness, new technology, and 24/7 news are contributing to journalism's rapidly changing role within the public sphere (Tumber and Prentoulis, 2003). The events of September 11, 2001 forced acknowledgement of changes in the micro and macro structures of war, including the significance of nation states. The emergence of terrorism as the dominant form of international conflict, and the need for the media to deal with the anxiety and trauma of unexpected attacks on ordinary citizens by unidentified 'aggressors', stimulated a demand that journalism develop an 'emotionally literate' engagement (Tumber and Prentoulis, 2003: 226–227).

Journalism's ideals of objectivity and critical reporting were substantially questioned by the events surrounding the reporting of the Gulf War in 2003. Military authorities heavily censored the reporting of correspondents, many of whom were 'embedded' within fighting units on the front line. This arguably served as a form of co-option. By presenting 'staged' press conferences and news releases, and briefing of combat personnel about how they should deal with the media, the coalition was able to achieve substantial control over the portrayal of events. The 24/7 news reporting of carefully crafted stories and accompanying visual images provided a form of reality television that attracted an audience of millions. Indeed, as Cooke notes, war shares the same language as theatre and sports and 'The interchangeability of the languages from these three domains blurs the distinctions so that the participation in war loses its own reality to be replaced by the glory of the spectacle or the competition' (1993: 182). This blurring was strongly evident during the news portrayal of the Gulf War of 2003 when news commentators provided a blow-by-blow account of events as they unfolded, 24 hours a day, seven days per week, showing graphic images of attacks such as the 'Shock and Awe' bombing campaign against Baghdad. By use of news commentary by 'reporters on the ground', news channels were able to provide audiences with an engaging and highly visual form of entertainment experienced at a safe distance from the actual events. A television documentary, *The War We Never Saw: The True*

Face of War, released a few months after the fall of Baghdad by UK's BBC4, provided some insight into the events and issues that audiences never saw, including the US military's threatening and abusive behaviour towards independent reporters. Like the portrayal of other aspects of the war, the portrayal of gender was far from neutral and was consistent with the gender hierarchies of news production in general (Rodgers, 2003).

Kill 'em all

The invasion of Iraq, led by US and UK troops in March 2003, generated some potent images of gender, particularly male gender, and emotional expression. A content analysis of news articles appearing in *The Guardian* newspaper, undertaken by the author for the weeks following the invasion, including stories of the 'liberation' of Baghdad, revealed predominant images of men and masculinity, particularly among US and UK soldiers, in various combat or evidently 'aggressive' situations. Images of men in portrayals of warfare in news and other media are so pervasive that the fact of the 'masculinisation' of war seems a self-evident truth that rarely warrants comment. One especially potent image, appearing on the front page, was of a US marine with a helmet on which was inscribed 'Kill 'em all', along with a demon-like figure and a skull and cross-bones. The accompanying article explains that,

> The marines have brought the whole encyclopaedia of military technology with them to Iraq. From aircraft to x-ray machines, they have a myriad ways to kill, heal wounded, survey, spy, reconnoitre, communicate with each other, shell, defend, attack, enfilade. They have brought all the machines and all the skilled people trained to use them. The equipment necessary to talk to Iraqis, understand their problems and respond to their needs, however, seems to have been left on the quayside in California. (Meek, 2003a: 1)

The article goes on to explain that, even before a recent suicide attack on US troops, 'the response of marines towards Iraqi civilians has been characterised by fear, suspicion, and mistrust' (Meek, 2003a: 1). This fear of the other and mistrust of, and lack of effort to understand and communicate with the other is a common response of combatants and, in fact, is instilled in soldiers, as a valued emotional trait. It is easier to kill a fellow human being if one loses empathy for them, if they are seen as different, untrustworthy, and less-than-human. In times of war, the enemy is demonised, and simplified images of the enemy are created, often drawing on national stereo-types such as 'The Germans', 'The Russians, 'The Japanese, or 'The Iraqis' (Groebel and Hinde, 1989: 190). Very often, racist images are employed, or the enemy is made to appear animal-like. This demonising and de-humanising of the other is not something that is innate in humans but, as is explained below, is instilled through military training. Although it is a feature of the training of both male and female recruits, in many contemporary Western societies, this lack of concern or empathy for the other is widely seen as a trait that is quintessentially 'masculine'.

The image of the warrior – the fearless individual who is ever ready for battle and prepared for sacrifice – figures prominently in news media images of warfare. It appears in many Western conceptions of masculinity and has provided an archetype for those who look to a mythical past to find valued models of contemporary manhood, such as in the mythopoetic men's movement (e.g. Bly, 1990). In the news media of the Gulf War, readers were presented with images of soldiers who coated their faces in warpaint before advancing into Baghdad (Meek, 2003b: 3). In one article, a reporter notes,

> The Cuban was the driver, the least painted-up of the Combined Anti-Armour Team Humvee that carried his name. Every other US marine in the car had coated his face in black and green warpaint in preparation for yesterday's entry into Baghdad. Eric the medic had painted his eyes black with stars like a clown, and blackened his lips so they spread across his chops from side to side. Staff Sergeant Jeff Fowler had completely blackened the bottom of his face, up to halfway up his nose, the top half remaining its natural pink. 'This is not the face of a peacekeeper', he said. 'I'm doin' the whole Last of the Mohicans kinda thing' . . .

This, and other transformative rituals such as taking drugs or lengthy drilling, to induce comradeship and an altered psychological state, are a common preliminary to killing and raping in war (Ehrenreich,

1997: 12). The ritual of face-painting, an aspect of many traditional communities, may to some seem childish and unnecessary in the modern theatre of war, characterised as it is by the use of sophisticated technologies and less face-to-face combat than in the past. However, it can be viewed as part of a repertoire of practices, including the continuing use of the bayonet and the bayonet charge, for keeping alive through performance the warrior myth that has been central to modern Western conceptions of masculinity (Bourke, 1999: 44–68). The above soldier's comments about 'doin' the whole Last of the Mohicans kinda thing' shows his acute recognition of the significance of the ritual of face-painting in the warrior myth.

In her study, Bourke reports that combatants in the First World War 'employed the language of chivalric ideals to describe their actions'; for example, bayonet fighting was described by one source as bringing back the 'barbaric nobility of war' (Bourke, 1999: 58). In modern warfare, however, the opportunities for demonstrating chivalry are often limited, especially when the enemy refuses or is unable to fight. In the case of Iraq, as it turned out, the US troops met little resistance on their entry to Baghdad, and were thus offered no opportunity to perform heroic acts. As one US marine, Major Andy Milburn was reported, 'It's kind of anti-climactic, isn't it? I thought it'd be a little different. It's not the liberation of Paris' (Meek, 2003b: 3). Despite the vastly superior military technology of the US–UK coalition that, for many commentators, made conquest over the Iraqi army highly predictable, readers are presented with a fairly conventional narrative of conquest, heroic acts and heroes. On the front page of the above edition of *The Guardian* newspaper, a group of soldiers – the 'liberators' – are seen in victorious posture in the presidential palace in Baghdad. One is sitting in a chair with his legs apart in stereotypically masculine pose and drawing on a cigarette in a self-satisfied gesture. An article appearing below it notes that the US troops 'smashed' the Iraqi Republican Guard and that,

> The aim of the incursion [into Baghdad] by 65 tanks and 40 armoured vehicles was both military and psychological....The US stronghold could serve as a temporary base from which to mount patrols and gather intelligence, but it was also intended to illustrate the vulnerability of Saddam Hussein's regime'. (Borger and McCarthy, 2003: 1)

The story conveyed here, and in other articles appearing during this brief war, was one of 'good' confronts 'evil', heroes versus cowards, and of 'good wins out'. The widely publicised images of Sadam Hussein's statue being pulled down provides one of the final symbolic gestures of 'liberation' (the toppling of a dictator), despite any physical evidence of the leader himself and any formal declaration of surrender or an end to the conflict.

Mostly absent from these mass-mediated images was any portrayal of women, either as combatants or 'behind the scenes', in supporting roles, or in the various forums of resistance, which emerged in the lead up to and during the war. A very different image of women and war is presented by Jenny Matthews' *Women and War*, a photo-documentary analysis covering twenty years from numerous war zones, including Iraq (Matthews, 2003). In this book, women are shown in diverse roles – as combatants, as carers, and as victims – and in relation to the particular conditions that confront them and their children following the outbreak and aftermath of war. Women were portrayed by the news media during the 2003 Gulf War largely as victims of war. That is, they appear as civilians, or as captives, who were heroically 'saved' by their male comrades – as in the case of Jessica Lynch, whose 'rescue', as it turned out, was scripted for the media. A similar gender biased news coverage pertained to the earlier events of September 11, when men were constructed as heroes and women as victims. The use of language in news reports in the immediate aftermath of the attack, such as the 'heroic fire*men*', served to diminish the roles of female officers and to reinforce the image of man as active and woman as passive (Rodgers, 2003: 206–208). The frequent invisibility of women and images of femininity in military institutions and the theatres of war has been a consistent feature of news reporting and public discourse about warfare in the modern period. However, the degree of the visibility of women and femininity is by no means invariant across time and place.

Women, the military, and emotion

Women's involvement and public visibility in the military, and particularly in combat roles in war, has varied considerably through history and across nations. Major factors affecting participation are the military's need for personnel and cultural values supporting gender equality (Segal, 1995). As Segal explains, women comprise a kind of reserve labour that is called upon in times of need. At such times, the history of women's involvement in war is used to show that they can perform effectively in various situations. However, in the aftermath of war, their military activities are reconstructed as minor or non-existent, thus allowing the perpetuation of the myth that there exists a distinct and invariable division of labour (Segal, 1995: 761). The type of role varies considerably, however, with it sometimes being depicted as an extension of the women's role as mothers protecting their children. (As Segal observes, women's participation is likely to be greater in peacekeeping and disaster-relief operations, and in operations that resemble domestic police functions [1995: 762].) While there has been a tendency to resist women's participation in 'risky' situations, particularly front-line duties, which may result in a large number of women casualties, women have and do take on such roles in certain circumstances. Changing military technology, demographic factors (including shortages of qualified men), labour force characteristics, economic variables, family roles, and social values all affect the degree of women's representation and the kinds of roles they undertake (Segal, 1995: 762–771). However, even when they are used marginally, their participation has been the source of public anxieties to a degree that is disproportionate to their actual numbers. For example, such anxiety was evident during the 1990–91 Gulf War (Enloe, 1994: 81). Consequently, when women have fought in a war zone, military commanders have been acutely sensitive about media coverage of women soldiers (Enloe, 1994: 99–102).

The evidence that exists suggests that women who undertake military roles act and respond in many respects like men in such roles. They are able to kill and to express feelings of comradeship and fear. In other words, there is nothing intrinsic to their biological sex that makes them immune to the kinds of action, thinking and feeling generally associated with male combatants. Although women are frequently refused access to the front lines, they have often demanded combat training and have taken the initiative in learning how to fire weapons. They have also played an active and apparently willing role in the weapons industry, including the Manhattan Project, in which women were involved in all technical aspects of the development of the atomic bomb (Howes and Herzenberg, 1993). There is a long history of women posing and passing as men in order to more actively participate at the front line and many historical narratives about women's pleasures in killing and in participating in military pursuits (e.g. Bourke, 1999: 306–314; Young, 1996). Of course, the question of whether women act as violently as men in similar situations of conflict is difficult to determine. Although, unlike men, women have not used rape as a weapon of control as have men, under certain historical and socio-political circumstances they would seem to have the potential to commit a similar level of violence. Some Palestinian suicide bombers have been women. Like male soldiers, many women are prepared to sacrifice themselves and others for 'the nation' or for a political or religious ideal. Also like male soldiers who have been described as transferring their love and desire for women to their weapons (see Bourke, 1999: 144; Theweleit, 1989: 170–172), women soldiers are known to develop a strong emotional attachment to their weapons. Women can be trained and can train themselves for 'combat readiness' by learning to empathise with their weapons. An Iranian women soldier, who is part of a resistance group (of which 70 per cent of the commanders are female) based in Iraq, describes her experiences thus:

> Here [in Iraq] I'm a gunner on a tank – in the past that was unimaginable – when I first saw a tank I thought how can this monster move? I was frightened when the guns were fired near me. At first it was difficult to lift tank shells. The noise in the turret, the smoke – it was all very alien and difficult, but eventually the tank became like putty in my hands and it got so my heart started to throb when I heard the tank engine. (Matthews, 2003: 11)

The initial sense of unfamiliarity, anxiety, and fear about the machinery of war described by this female soldier is often depicted in popular discourse as a characteristically feminine response. The expressed fear of the weapons themselves and the reported physical difficulty of dealing with the armaments are thus not unexpected responses. However, as the soldier's comments suggest, women, too, can learn to control, and indeed 'love' their weapon and feel a similar sense of exhilaration when the weapon is engaged.

Despite women's demonstrated ability to perform and respond much like men when in combat roles, it has been consistently argued that women are innately different in ways that justifies their exclusion from combat roles. As Bourke observes, during the First and Second World Wars, 'administrative, strategic, and ideological arguments were put forward to keep women out of combat' (1999: 335). It was argued that, in battle, duplicating accommodation and sanitary facilities in order to maintain separate access for the two sexes would be expensive and present difficulties in practical maintenance. Further, the rational allocation of 'manpower' was seen to necessitate an economical and effective division of labour, whereby women, who were not yet required in the trenches, were needed to help men who were in the trenches (Bourke, 1999: 335–336). However, 'the primary arguments against arming women were explicitly political and ideological, though this varied from country to country' (Bourke, 1999: 337). During these wars and since, those who have sought to exclude women from combat roles have contended that women are unsuited to combat roles because they have different emotional and physical capacities and present a disruptive influence.

Such arguments were evident, for example, in the long-awaited UK report, *Women in the Armed Forces*, which was released in 2000 (MoD, 2002). Drawing on a range of information, including a survey of the scientific literature, and 'the results of a field exercise to explore the impact of mixed gender teams on cohesion and military performance', the report concluded that women should continue to be barred from close combat roles (MoD, 2002: 2). The report noted that 'the capacity for aggression ... was generally lower for women, who required more provocation and were more likely to fear the consequences of aggressive behaviour'. It also commented that women had a lesser 'capacity to develop muscle strength and aerobic fitness ... such that only approximately 1 per cent of women can equal the performance of the average man' and had a 'lower work capacity'. Further, it cited some published evidence that 'the inclusion of small numbers of women adds to the difficulty of creating the necessary degree of cohesion' in combat teams. It noted that this evidence 'found that the attitudes of group members, particularly positive and negative attitudes to gender and gender stereotypes, could affect group dynamics and ultimately group effectiveness'. Consequently, 'it might be easier to achieve and maintain cohesion in a single sex team' (MoD, 2002: 3). Finally, it noted that although there was some other evidence to show that 'under normal conditions ... the presence of women in small units does not affect performance detrimentally', 'there is no evidence to show whether this remains under the extreme conditions of high intensity close combat' (MoD, 2002: 4).

> The reality of warfighting is that the combat team must function effectively over an extended period in conditions that are character-ised by extreme danger, confusion, fatigue and noise. There is no way of knowing whether mixed gender teams can function as well as all-male teams in a close combat environment. Empirical evidence on this subject cannot be obtained, as there is no way to replicate the conditions of close combat by any means short of risking our forces in battle. (MoD, 2002: 4)

Women have long been excluded from combat in a number of countries, including the UK and the US, on the basis that they may threaten the cohesion of the fighting group. This view has gained much support from the male-bonding hypothesis, first popularised by Lionel Tiger. In his book, *Men in Groups* (1969), Tiger argued that 'male bonding' is a biologically based behaviour that plays a significant role in human society (Goldstein, 2001: 195). Tiger believed that small, select groups worked to reaffirm male solidarity by 'degrading the male–female bond', which evidently explains men's misogynistic behaviour and why it is difficult for women to participate in all-male contexts, including war. On the basis of this theory, Tiger predicted that women would not be able to participate in combat, become armed police officers, or become political leaders in significant numbers. Yet, women's participation in policing and in politics has increased significantly, while female participation in combat has lagged, which presents a difficulty for his theory (Goldstein, 2001: 195).

The continuing exclusion of women from combatant roles on the grounds of their different capacities or abilities is curious in the light of broader shifts in views about women's participation in public life in general, reflected in equal opportunities legislation. The Sex Dis-crimination Act (1975), however, makes an exception in the case of the Armed Forces, which are permitted to exclude women from those posts 'where the military judgement is that the employment of women would undermine and degrade combat effectiveness'. This is a policy that was upheld by the European Court of Justice in 1999 (MoD, 2002: 4). The focus on combat roles is also difficult to under-stand given the increasing blurring of the boundaries between combat and non-combat in modern warfare (Morgan, 1994: 170, 176). This blurring of roles was evident, for example, in the US Army in the 1990–91 Gulf War, which involved an historically high number of women. Forty thousand white, black, and Asian-American women were deployed in Saudi Arabia during the nine-month military build up – four times the number of American military women sent to Vietnam during the decade of US involvement in that war (Enloe, 1994: 81). As Morgan notes, the distinction between combat and non-combat is dynamic and fluid and individuals may move between such roles according to circumstances. Many discussions of women in combat fail to distinguish between offensive and defensive combat roles, and assume that many women are currently non-combatants and that a policy shift to assigning them to offensive positions will necessarily change their status to combatants (Segal, 1982: 268–269). The distinction between combat and non-combat roles is especially difficult to sustain in the case of 'peacekeeping' and 'counter-terrorism' activities, which are not strictly offensive roles but may involve extreme danger.

After the release of the above Ministry of Defence report, the Deputy Chairwoman of the Equal Opportunities Commission drew attention to the equal opportunities implications of women's exclusion from combat roles. In a news article she noted, 'automatically excluding women is not the right approach...and each woman should be judged on the basis of their ability to carry out the job, using relevant tests' (Norton-Taylor, 2002: 6). However, this held no weight with defence officials who, in response, argued that 'old arguments about chivalry played no part' in the decision and that, in fact, 'women had had a "civilising effect" on the armed forces and had improved discipline on board Royal Navy ships'. As the chief of defence staff pointed out, 'his main concern was that women infantry, wounded or killed in battle, would affect their male colleagues in a way that would disrupt military operations' (Norton-Taylor, 2002: 6). Although not spelt out, the assumption here seems to be that the potential for the enactment of traditional gender roles, which prescribes that men should be the protectors and women as the protected, would lead to a breakdown in group solidarity and hence detract from the military mission. In other words, what is fundamentally at issue in relation to women's participation in combat roles, it seems, is the perceived threat that women pose to the established gender relations of power. They are perceived as a potentially threatening influence and therefore in need of exclusion from particularly 'risky' roles or at least limitation to roles where the risks are limited or less immediate. The argument that women present a potential disruption to 'combat effectiveness' and should therefore be excluded from direct combat roles is not new. For example, in the early 1980s, an ex-infantry officer in the US Army argued that, 'even if women were physically equal or superior to men', their integration would likely adversely affect 'the cohesion and fighting qualities of the combat group' (Tuten, 1982: 252). As this writer commented, it is difficult to assess the effect of women on combat effectiveness since 'the sustained stress of actual combat cannot be duplicated'. In the absence of such knowledge the inclusion of women involves the risk that the combat effectiveness of mixed units will be reduced. Further, 'it is highly unlikely that the extent of such a combat capability degradation can be known before it is too late to reverse it or overcome its consequences' (Tuten, 1982: 252). There is a striking similarity between the argument used here and that used in the *Women in the Armed Forces* report (MoD, 2002), cited above, published twenty years later. The issues that are presented to support women's exclusion from combat roles – their differences in 'capacity for aggression', their differences in physical ability, and their unpredictable responses under pressure and potentially disruptive behaviour – have been raised in arguments in the past to justify women's exclusion from many fields of employment. Sometimes the claims are difficult to substantiate, as admitted above in relation to the effect of mixed gender teams on combat effectiveness, on other occasions they are supported by reference to supposedly objective science.

As indicated in the last chapter, the idea that women and men have 'different capacities for aggression' has a long history in the psychology of aggression. Despite shifts in theories of aggression, with different theories giving somewhat different weight to the relative influences of 'nature' and 'nurture', the idea that there is an innate or biological difference between 'the sexes' has been enduring. This argument, along with claims that women have different physical capacities that make them unsuitable for certain tasks, is consistent with the 'two-sex' model that has dominated thinking in the Western world since the Enlightenment (Laqueur, 1990). However, the idea that women are inferior or are the 'weaker seed' has a much longer history, stretching back to the period of the ancient Greeks (Schiebinger,

1989: 160–165). The notion of two fundamentally different, but complementary, sexes, with women being seen as the 'gentler sex', has been used to justify women's exclusion from public life, including politics, medicine, law, and the military. In the history of modern medicine, the notion of an essential or innate difference has been invoked in arguments for excluding women from undertaking anatomical dissection, seen as a rite of passage and a badge of identity for medical professionals. Women have been seen as unable to cope with the messiness, smell, and sight of dead bodies. And, the female presence in the dissecting room has been perceived as a threat to both the norms of male bonding and to notions of femininity (Sappol, 2002: 88–90). The argument that women should be excluded from combat on the grounds that they do not have the 'capacity for aggression', or are potentially a threatening or disruptive influence, or are unable to cope with the stresses of combat, can be seen as continuous with this history. There is no empirical evidence to support or refute the claim that women's presence will disrupt 'combat effectiveness'; however, the *belief* that this will occur serves as a self-fulfilling prophecy. As Segal argues, if men believe that women are not part of the group and they cannot function with women around, then this belief will disrupt such functioning and may hinder the ability to cope with the demands of combat (1982: 278). This same belief operates in relation to members of the gay community who have long been excluded from the institutions of the military.

That there is a great deal of resistance within the military to women's involvement in combat is supported by a recent study. This examined how women were presented in policy documentation produced by the Ministry of Defence and the Army aimed at facilitating women's inclusion, and included interviews with those who developed and implemented these policies (Woodward and Winter, 2003). It found that, although policies on equal opportunities and diversity had been developed, policy debates and practices reflect a number of circulating discourses about the woman soldier. That is, they are 'capable but limited, keen but sensible, sexualised, potentially disruptive, and potentially one of the male group but ultimately limited in her contribution because of her sex and physicality'. The researchers argue that 'these military cultural constructions make the figure of the woman soldier safe, contained and unthreatening' which 'could be interpreted as a defensive act, a cultural mechanism for protecting the Army as a masculine institution' (Woodward and Winter, 2003: 5). Further, the study also noted a recent, subtle shift away from the language of equal opportunities to talk about 'managing diversity'. This shift, the researchers argued, fitted with the Army's values, which emphasised fairness and the valuing of the individual's contribution to a larger team, but overlooked the power relations that underlie the construction of difference (Woodward and Winter, 2003: 8). As they commented,

> Diversity, for women soldiers, allows their incorporation into the Army, but only insofar as they can be like men and conform to the group. Military discourses about gender construct women as different in specific ways; some of these differences are presented as incompatible with military life, and problematic to women's full inclusion in the Army. (Woodward and Winter, 2003: 9)

The view that women are temperamentally ill suited to the demands of military life, or share anti-war values, also finds support *outside* the institutions of the military. Many writers, including feminist scholars, have argued that women lack aggressivity or the 'killer instinct' and/ or are innately more peace loving, gentler, and more empathetic and caring than men. The links between femininity and pacifism and between masculinity and aggressivity has been a recurring motif in battle narratives. Despite recent efforts to challenge this dichotomy, discussions which posit a strict separation between male and female 'spheres' have prevailed (Bourke, 1999: 309–312). Some feminists cite evidence of women's greater involvement in pacifist activities, or draw attention to strong historical links between feminist and pacifist movements (e.g. Costin, 1982; Marquit and Marquit, 1991; Seitz, *et al.*, 1993; Stephenson, 1982; Washburn, 1993). Women's involvement in organised efforts for peace, for example during the First World War or more recently Greenham Common, is seen by some writers as confirming the intrinsic links between pacifism and femininity (Costin, 1982: 305). According to Warren, an eco-feminist scholar, 'sexism is intimately connected to other "isms of domination," e.g. racism, classism, heterosexism, militarism; ecological feminists have extended these analyses to include "naturism," or the unjustified exploitation of the natural environment' (1994: 181). 'Women', like 'nature' has become 'other', something different from the dominant, and have been similarly objectified and subordinated (King, 1989: 21). The commonality between the feminist and pacifist movements, it is argued, is the rejection of the 'male value system', with the focus on power and domination; that is, 'power over or against' (Stephenson, 1982: 291).

According to a common strand of feminist thought, war and militarism cannot be disconnected from the broader pervasive structure of power: 'patriarchy'. The authors of one article, for instance, write:

> war and militarism foster and legitimize the prevailing system of patriarchal power, and they model and legitimate violence as an acceptable technique for achieving social objectives. Military training and values are seen as applicable and useful in 'civilian' society at large. Indeed, military ability – which, presumably, means the ability to commit physical violence – is a major component of many males' gender identification. Masculinity is seen as primary to war and militarism; in fact, it has been *defined* by an ability to learn the necessary techniques of war. And because of its perceived importance, this ability is reproduced and enforced by a whole range of influences (parents, schools, and sports, for example), consciously or unconsciously, in successful generations of children. Second, under patriarchy, women are coerced and encouraged to collaborate with the military on many levels, and women's wide participation is absolutely necessary for its continuance.... (Dorsch, *et al.*, 1991: 140)

For pacifists, non-violence means a rejection of direct and structural violence and opposition to oppression whether based on sexism, racism, or other ideology. Some feminists argue that these are values which are held more by women than by men, although they may disagree about whether this is due to 'nature' or 'nurture' (Stephenson, 1982: 291). In some strands of eco-feminism, women are portrayed as more connected with 'life', 'nature' and the 'cosmos' and thus are the 'natural' guardians of the planet. The implication, sometimes articulated, often not, is that men are 'destroyers' and 'exploiters'. Phrases such as 'healing the wounds' and 'reweaving the world', which draw strongly on imagery pertaining to women's traditional caring and creative roles, are sometimes used to emphasise women's stronger affinity to 'life' and 'nature' (see, e.g. Diamond and Orenstein,

1990). Occasionally, feminists and biological theorists converge in their 'essentialist' accounts of war. That is, in explaining warfare, they attribute a universal nature to human beings – explained either by 'nurture' or 'nature' – thus denying the variations that exist among them (Oyama, 1991: 64).

Survey data and other supposedly 'hard' empirical evidence (e.g. criminal statistics) are sometimes cited to support claims about 'essential' sex differences in views on, and propensity to participate in, war. One common source of data is surveys exploring women's and men's levels of support for the use of military force in times of war or imminent war. In the aftermath of the September 11 terrorist attacks in New York, the findings of a poll of 3000 people were published by *The Observor* showing that British women were less inclined to support the use of military force in the 'war on terrorism' than men. The news report noted that, 'Three quarters of men back air strikes, but this falls to 55 per cent among women.' Further, 'Fifty three per cent of men believe Britain should commit troops to the "war against terrorism", but it is a view shared by only 36 per cent of women . . .' (Summerskill, 2001: 5). Analyses of such surveys, some spanning large periods of time, reveal that men are more inclined than women to favour the direct use of force in resolving international conflict (see Gallagher, 1993). Such data is frequently cited to support the view of a 'gender gap' in attitudes to the use of force in specific situations and is assumed to reflect different gender orientations towards the use of aggression or violence. However, there are many problems associated with the use and analysis of surveys. A major limitation is their use of simple snap shot measures of attitudes ('yes/approve', 'not opposed', and 'don't know'). It is often difficult to know whether attitudinal differences between the sexes are greater or smaller than differences within each group, and why respondents chose as they did (Gallagher, 1993: 30). As Gallagher argues, it is crucial to know whether or not those who oppose force do so because they believe it is unnecessary, ineffective, or inappropriate to the issue at hand. Surveys often use leading questions and simplify issues that are complex (1993: 30–31). Survey questions are often ambiguous and provide little insight into the relationship between views expressed and dispositions and actions. Surveys are likely to reveal more about the assumptions held by researchers than about any 'real' difference among those who are surveyed.

Military training and the forging of identities

Military training would seem to play a crucial role in engendering differences, by effecting change in the identities and dispositions of recruits as well as serving, symbolically, to differentiate the 'strong' or 'fit', who are defined by reference to a particular ideal of masculinity, and the 'weak' or 'unfit', who implicitly are equated with femininity. For the male gender, it is a rite de passage both from civilian to infantryman and from boyhood to manhood. As Jonathan Glover explains, 'Military training has to make people do things which they would not do in civilian life' (2001: 51). It erodes civilian identity and values. This is helped by psychological remoteness from ordinary life and through the infliction of physical and verbal abuse and humiliation (Glover, 2001: 51). The various ordeals undertaken by recruits – the drill, circuit training, road runs, assault courses, and forced speed marches carrying loads of equipment – are an indicator of the individual's masculinity and this point is repeatedly reinforced by the instructional staff (Hockey, 2003: 16). While positive performances are praised by training staff as evidence of masculinity, the failure to perform is often equated with femininity and is portrayed as weak and is the cause of derogatory comments from instructors. Recruits are taught to be aggressive and 'lack of aggression is ... correlated with femininity, inadequacy, and, ultimately and quite fundamentally with death' (Hockey, 2003: 16–17). What is at issue in this endeavour to shape bodies and minds is the stability of the symbolic order, in particular the linkages between masculinity and violence. As Morgan argues:

> In the cases of the military, the kinds of issues that are at stake here include the extent to which women, especially in a combat situation, might be defined as weakening or polluting; the extent to which feminine skills or aptitudes for caring and nurturing will be diminished through such participations; as well as the more openly expressed questions as to whether women would be able to cope with the rigors and deprivations of war and training. Other major concerns have been whether men will obey women officers and whether men will endanger themselves by protecting women in combat situations. But running through all these concerns and coloring them at every point is a concern

with the overall symbolic order, the apparent loosening of boundaries between women and men, and the weakening of the links between nation, the military, and gendered identities. (Morgan, 1994: 171)

In Morgan's view, the linkages between masculinity, violence, and the military, although providing some of the most potent images of gender in many cultures, is far from straightforward (Morgan, 1994: 179). Indeed, it is a cultural achievement that is constantly threatened by women's presence, especially in what are considered traditional masculine domains, such as combat roles. Hence, changes in the gender order invariably have an effect on how the military is conceived and constructed (Morgan, 1994: 180).

In her book, *The Intimate History of Killing: Face-to-Face Killing in Twentieth-Century Warfare*, Joanna Bourke, emphasises the importance of training men to kill in modern warfare. As Bourke explains, with reference to examples from the First World War, the Second World War, and the Vietnam War, motivating men to kill has not been an easy task. Thus a chief function of military training has been to instil into recruits such military traits as toughness, alertness, loyalty and discipline (1999: 72). Officers in the front lines have repeatedly expressed concerns about the success of training in terms of motivating men to fight. Studies confirm that only a proportion of combatants ever fire their weapons in battle, even when they are within easy firing distance of the enemy, and that of those who fire often only a small proportion hit their targets (Bourke, 1999: 74–75). According to Bourke, this inhibition on killing is explained, at least in part, by the changing technologies and personnel of warfare. The increasing use of sophisticated technology, which separated opposing combatants from each other, rendered redundant earlier methods for ensuring that men would fight. Those on the battlefield often did not directly confront the enemy and combants reported seeing no one and thus feeling 'unnerved' by the feeling of 'fighting phantoms'. The feeling of isolation and confusion in battle experienced by soldiers mitigated against them 'acting aggressively'. Also, by the middle of the First World War, officers were no longer 'socialised warriors' who had experienced long periods of training in military colleges. They could not be depended on to act promptly in times of need, a problem exacerbated by the increasing difficulty of motivating soldiers to 'hate' the enemy. The use of the negative incentives of punishment and fear were less effective among reluctant servicemen who regarded dismissal from the armed services in a positive light. Consequently, recruits were subjected to 'hate training', which involved the resocialisation of individuals into efficient fighting men. This included various forms of brutalisation, such as depersonalisation, lack of privacy, uniforms, forced social relationships, tight schedules, sleep deprivation, 'disorientation followed by rites of reorganization according to military codes', arbitrary rules and strict punishment (Bourke, 1999: 79). 'These forms of brutalisation were similar to those carried out in regimes where men were taught to torture prisoners: the difference resided in the *degree* of violence involved, not its *nature*' (Bourke, 1999: 79; emphases in original).

As Bourke notes, psychology has played a key role in military training, in desensitising recruits to the noise and gore of battle, in instilling or encouraging particular character traits (particularly the instinct of aggression), and in engendering group solidarity (1999: 96–102). The formation of male identity through military training goes hand in hand with the denigration of women and their exclusion from particular military roles. Bourke (1999) has described the significance of male bonding for the nurturance and utilisation of particular emotions needed by combatants. Love and hate play complementary parts in training recruits to kill. The combatants in Bourke's study reported that they were able to kill because of the love they felt for their comrades. Stories of immense love for one's comrades-in-arms and 'homo-erotic relationships' have recurred in literature on men's experiences of war. 'Brotherly love' has been encouraged among servicemen, and the military establishment has rhetorically evoked the symbolic parent to entice men to kill (Bourke, 1999: 139–151). The exclusivity of the combat unit is sustained through the de-humanisation of socially subordinated groups. The vicious treatment of certain groups, including women, is perceived to reinforce in-group identity and to prepare troops for combat readiness by de-humanising the enemy (Harrison, 2003: 75). As Harrison argues, the military constructs the polarity of masculine and feminine in order to unite 'real' military men and to distinguish them from non-masculine men and women. Very few in the military community challenge the dichotomy between 'tougher warrior' men and supportive 'dependent' women. During training, recruits are encouraged to adopt stereotypical masculine behaviours and female-associated words are used to derogate them. Male recruits earn the right to be addressed as 'men'. Especially macho groups objectify women by viewing pornographic films, and joking about making women the targets of violence. Dehumanising women and members of ethnic minorities serve simultaneously to unite combat units and to make troops 'combat ready' (Harrison, 2003: 75).

According to the prevailing psychological view of the Second World War, if men were to prove effective combatants, they needed to be lavished with fatherly affection. As Bourke explains,

> A combatant's desire to please his father was largely unconscious... and was based upon strong love and affection developed in early life. The most important factor in the process of identification was the assurance that he was adored by a man wielding considerable authority. When this occurred, the desire to conform to the demands of the group become almost irresistible. The 'father' had to be strong, decisive and technically competent so that his men would feel protected. He had to demonstrate good judgement and had to play the role of a 'just and impartial father', rewarding and punishing men appropriately. So long as the soldier retained strong ties of affection for the group and identified with its ideals, he would be protected from overpowering anxiety and would be able to kill without qualm. (Bourke, 1999: 145)

In Bourke's view, this emphasis on familial ties extended further, to include those who were the enemy. Combatants at the front lines often expressed respect for their opponents and even fraternised with them on occasion, particularly during religious holidays. The dual imperative to love and to hate created ambivalent feelings towards one's foes (Bourke, 1999: 146–148). Thus, emotion needed to be closely policed and channelled: 'hatred might reduce "combat effectiveness", love might enhance it' (Bourke, 1999: 168). With technological innovations, the value of passion in warfare decreased: chronic aggressiveness worked against the ideals of teamwork and the co-ordination needed to complete tasks. Keeping the emotions 'in check' was essential to establishing confidence in the political aims of the war and diminishing the psychological conflict over killing (Bourke, 1999: 168).

The significance of the military for the forging of masculine identities varies between societies and within societies through time. In some, the military plays a central role in the rite de passage to male adulthood. In Israeli society the Army is the main mechanism for building a national identity, while for male youths, the military service is an inherent part of maturation and provides entry into the public sphere (Klein, 2003). While both women and men are drafted, in percentage terms males have a higher rate of entry into the military and are much more likely to complete the required 24 months. The military serves as a kind of sorting mechanism, for defining who is 'in' and who is 'out' with respect to the collective and the informal system (Klein, 2003: 191). It is a bodily experience and a means of disciplining and shaping bodies, and of separating boys and girls, as well as a vehicle for nurturing emotional control. Learning to fight means, first and foremost, to control feelings of fear. As Klein points out, in Hebrew the verb *lehitgaber* means 'to overcome' or 'to get over' which is based on the same root as *gever*, 'man'. Further, *gibor*, 'the hero', is derived from *gever* (2003: 196). In the former German Democratic Republic, the military played a similar role in the formation of male identity; however, in addition, mandatory military training and military service for men fulfilled a key ideological role in transmitting the ideological and political aims of the Socialist United Party (Bickford, 2003). Again, military service served as a means of categorising, sorting, and subjugating persons: '"citizens" were coded as men conducting (or who had conducted) military service, whereas "girls" and "women" remained something outside the "true" citizenship and, in extreme cases, outside of "humanity"' (Bickford, 2003: 162).

The significance of language

As the above suggests, in the military context, language is crucial in engendering difference, serving both symbolically to demarcate the masculine from the feminine and in socialising initiates into gendered ways of thinking and acting. By learning a specific language, recruits come to share a perspective on the social world and to respond to events in a similar way. That language is gendered has long been recognised by feminist scholars. In her seminal book, *Man Made Language* (1980), Dale Spender drew attention to the sexual politics of language.

As Spender observed, language has a male bias that makes women appear deficient or deviant. This does not necessarily occur as the result of the conscious effort of men to exclude women but rather through the taken-for-granted assumption 'that the world is male unless proven otherwise' (Spender, 1980: 20). Feminist linguists have explored how masculinity is enacted through language, and manifest in the organisation of talk, in the adoption of particular speech styles, in practices of naming, and in the use of particular narratives and vocabulary (see, e.g. Johnson and Meinhof, 1997). In the institutions of the military and in times of war, narrative conventions prescribe that certain acts are 'masculine' or 'feminine', regardless of who performs them.

> In any given war, a military participant may at one time lead troops against an enemy position and at other times peel potatoes, dig latrines, polish boots, or treat a buddy's frostbitten feet. Conventional military history will describe a man who does these things as a 'soldier'. If a woman does the same things, historical sources, if they notice her at all, will probably refer to her as a 'nurse'. If the male soldier has a lover or a family, it will make no difference to the historical record, but the woman will be placed in a sexually defined category to the exclusion of any others. These are the literary conventions; no matter how heroic and 'manly' a woman may be, narrative conventions will deny her gallantry and emphasize her nurturing qualities and sensitivity. He is stalwart and brave; she is cute when she is angry.... (De Pauw, 1998: 17)

In military settings, language signifies gender most directly in the speech act: 'speaking like a man'. It is also manifest in the interpretation of another's acts, such as 'acting like a wimp'. Such language contributes to gender discourse, which comprises 'a system of meanings, ways of thinking, images and words that first shape how we experience, understand, and represent ourselves as men and women' as well as other aspects of our lives (Cohen, 1993: 229). As Cohen (1993) explains, in this symbolic system, human characteristics are divided into dichotomies such as mind versus body, culture versus nature, thought versus feeling, logic versus intuition, which are associated with male and female, respectively. Further, each of these binary oppositions corresponds with a system of valuation, whereby one side of the binary – the male – is valued over the second – the female. In gender discourse, men and women are expected to exemplify the respective characteristics in the list; alternatively, evidence of these characteristics – to be abstract, rational, and dispassionate – is not simply to be those things but to be 'manly' (Cohen, 1993: 229). Displaying such characteristics also positions one within the gender discourse: it associates one with a particular gender and with it a higher or lower evaluation. As Cohen emphasises, this is a symbolic system in that few men and women neatly fit with these ideals, but it nonetheless affects all of us, in that we see and evaluate ourselves and others against its templates (Cohen, 1993: 229). Thus, a man who cries cannot avoid confronting that he is likely to be seen as less than manly. Expressing emotions that are associated with the opposite gender are likely to be met with opprobrium and exclusion. Male soldiers who express uncontrolled emotional outbursts, such as empathy or concern for the enemy, are marked not only as unprofessional but also as feminine and in the devalued or subordinate position in the gender discourse (Cohen, 1993: 231). Any act of supposed weakness or behaviour that is associated with the opposite gender is likely to be derided, and soldiers who transgress expected gender roles are vulnerable to 'gender bashing'. Derogatory terms are often sexually connoted, as in 'pussy', which joins 'the imagery of harmless domesticated (read demasculined) with contemptuous reference to women's genitals' (Cohen, 1993: 235).

In her ethnographic study of defence intellectuals and their discussions of nuclear weapons, Cohen (1990) concluded that defence language performs an important role in distancing the speaker and listener from the realities of nuclear holocaust. It shields users from the emotional reaction that would ensue if it were clear that one were talking about plans for mass murder or genocide. For instance, the use of the term 'clean bombs', which are nuclear devices detonated by fusion rather than fission, and hence produce less radioactive fallout, denies the awful effects of these armaments (Cohen, 1990: 34). She also found that sexual and patriarchal imagery was rife in references to 'vertical erector launches', 'thrust-to-weight ratios', 'soft lay-downs', 'deep penetration', 'patting the missile', and so on. Finally, she discovered that 'talking about nuclear weapons was fun' and that she began to 'think in it' to the extent that it shaped her responses to new ideas. Like an anthropologist who has 'gone native', Cohen began to appreciate how learning military language was a transformative rather than an additive process. As she noted, 'When you choose to learn it you are not simply adding new information and vocabulary; you are entering into a particular mode of thinking about nuclear weapons, military and political power, and about the relationship between human ends and technological means' (Cohen, 1990: 50). In other words, by learning military language, one also produces gender discourse and all that that entails, including the distancing of the self from the other, the subordination of the feminine, and the privileging of the rational over the affective. Recognising this, those who are opposed to militarism and sexism have stressed the import-ance of attending to the politics of military language. In particular, a growing number of writers see it as important to explore how language serves to make certain ways of thinking seem natural and inevitable and to constrain the search for more peaceful means of resolving conflict.

Conclusion: gender, emotion, and the changing face of militarism and war

This chapter has focused on the associations between gender and emotion in the contexts of the military and warfare. It examined the mechanisms sustaining these associations, including media portrayals, military training, practices of exclusion, and the use of particular language. And, it highlighted the significance of theories, particularly Darwinian and Freudian theories, in explaining the origins of (male) aggression and war, in the training of soldiers, and in justifying the fact of war and the many atrocities (e.g. rape) committed during the course of battle. Such theories contribute to the discourse about gen-der and emotion, particularly aggressiveness, either through their implicit assumptions about innate differences or through explicit references to the different capacities of 'the sexes'. The analysis has been limited to the recent past and to empirical evidence from Western societies. What I have described are tendencies that are by no means unchangeable. Indeed, recognising the fact of change is crucial in allowing one to consider that things could be otherwise and how they might be different. The changing character of war, wrought by new global political forces and formations and new technologies, threatens to destabilise established discourses of gender and emotion. The growing significance of 'terrorism' as a political phenomenon (see Whittaker (2001: 3–13) for a discussion of some difficulties in defining the term 'terrorist'), challenges the connection between warfare, as a conflict between nation states, and aggressive masculinity, that has guided thinking and action for much of the modern period in the West. Increasing focus on women's participation in armed subversion in contexts of substantial socio-economic ine-quality and rapid social change (see, e.g. De Cataldo Neuburger and Valentini, 1996) further challenges cultural stereotypes about men's and women's natural roles and capacities. The rise of religious funda-mentalist movements and new local ethnic alliances, in both the developed and developing worlds, has been a significant challenge to the established global political order, which has been strongly based on class-based and nation-based affiliations and ideologies. These developments, regardless of how they are evaluated, serve to draw attention to the historical contingency of many categories, hierarchies, and associations. There is nothing inevitable about the links between aggressivity and masculinity and between passivity and femininity or about the privileging of rationality over emotionality. And, it is not inevitable that men and women enact their lives according to cultural prescriptions that pertain to bodies of designated sexes. This is not to deny physical difference, but rather to emphasise the historical variability in our ways of understanding and the significance of the social meanings that attach to the categories of identity that profoundly shape our lives. In order to highlight further the contin-gency of gender-emotion associations, the next chapter focuses attention on a domain that seems far removed from the contexts of the military and warfare; namely, love, intimacy, and sex.

4
Love, Intimacy, and Sex

Sorting the wheat from the chaff

You have spotted a virtual hunk, but how do you decide if he is the guy for you? Here is how to find the truth behind the profile.

Let's face it. Finding guys online isn't difficult. Log on to any chat room or online dating agency and you'll find the place stuffed to capacity with them. The question is, how do you separate the wheat from the chaff, or more simply, Prince Charming from Homer Simpson.

Before you even turn on your computer, sit yourself down and think about what you want to find in the first place. Unless you take a long, hard look at yourself there is no way you can successfully look for love. You may be looking for a knight in shining armour to sweep you off your feet and whisk you into a relationship of passion and adventure. Then again perhaps you only want a short-term fling. And there's nothing to be ashamed about being one of the growing number of people who just want to meet new friends.

Once you've narrowed your criteria into a clear picture of what you want then it's time to hit the profiles.... So, you've worked out what kind of person you want to find and are faced with a list of guys who match your requirements. What next? Well, hold off from sending that email or message just yet. The next step is to become an expert profile reader and there is only one way to achieve this: read, read and read some more.

Think about it for a second. You're off on a shoe buying expedition. The last thing you'll do is go for the first pair that catches your eye. No, you'll think about what pair goes with what outfit and then shop around, seeing what else is available or whether there are any bargains to be had. Why then would you swoop in on the first potential beau that you spot? To be able to separate the wheat from the chaff you need to learn how to read between the lines.... (*Connect magazine*, Autumn, 2003: 22–23)

The above excerpt, taken from an article in a magazine devoted to relationships and online dating, would seem to reveal much about changing gender roles and changing expectations in relation to meeting a member of the opposite sex. Although the piece is written in a light-hearted style intended to entertain as much as to inform, the idea that women may 'look for love' in such a calculating (predatory?) way, and choose a partner as one may choose a pair of shoes, seems to reverse a long-established view on male and female roles and behaviours; namely, that men initiate sexual relationships and objectify women. The sexual selection 'at a distance' that the Internet allows is novel, and tells us much about how a new technology of communication may allow the creation of new meanings concerning partner selection and love. The provision of this kind of 'how to do it' advice in relation to meeting a potential 'Mr Right' also seems far removed from what would have been considered acceptable in many, if not most societies until relatively recently. Increasingly, competent decision-making in matters of the heart, like decision-making in other areas of our lives, is seen as something that can be learnt and perfected in practice, so that one can see past the impression, to discover the 'genuine article'. That a specialist magazine has been created precisely for advice and information on the initiation of dating underlines the extent to which the mediation of relationships via such means has been 'normalised' in contemporary society. However, despite the shifting scripts of gender and rituals of sexual interaction between women and men, there is strong evidence to suggest that long-established assumptions about differences between the sexes and about the processes of sexual attraction have remained relatively stable.

This chapter focuses on the engendering of emotions in the sphere of love, intimacy, and sex, and assesses the extent to which recent apparent shifts in gender roles, the discourse of romantic love, and sexual rituals represent a challenge to dominant constructions of sex/gender difference. It explores the role of expertise and of consumerism in regulating intimate life, and how difference is generated and regulated in matters of the heart. The terms 'falling in love' and 'making love' have come to designate aspects of experience that seem quintessential to the human condition. Experts have in various ways sought to articulate the norms of love, intimacy, and sex, as though these dimensions of experience can be objectively known and their meaning and significance universally recognised. However, definitions of love, intimacy, and sex change through time and mirror the politics of prevailing constructions of gender and sexuality. Dominant notions of romantic love in the contemporary West embody a heterosexist bias and reflect and reinforce gender-specific assumptions about how men and women, respectively, *should* conduct themselves. The chapter begins by exploring the pervasive influence of the notion of romantic love, which provides the ideal for 'normal' relations between the sexes before moving on to examine in detail some mechanisms by which difference is produced and regulated. Finally, it considers and assesses the significance of some emergent practices of love, sex, and intimacy for contemporary constructions of masculinity and femininity.

The discourses of romantic love: governing matters of the heart

The topic of romantic love, of people 'falling in love', of 'making love', of 'passionate affairs', and of love gone awry or of 'falling out of love' has long been the subject of novels, television soap operas, news articles, and magazines oriented to a mass readership. In recent years, there has also been a burgeoning academic literature on the subject of love, with contributions from many disciplines, including biology, psychology, sociology, anthropology, and cultural studies. The mechanisms of love – what makes men and women mutually attractive – have been extensively explored by biologists and psychologists. Scholars have raised such questions as, what bio-chemical and psycho-social processes account for attraction between the sexes? And, do those of opposite disposition attract or do we come to love those who have a similar personality or 'temperament'? Social scientists, particularly historians, sociologists and anthropologists have examined the changing and contested concept of love itself, through time and across societies. The origins of romantic love, and the character and significance of the era which gave rise to this concept, have also been of increasing interest to scholars. Finally, sociologists have explored changes in the nature of love and of intimate relations in late modernity, including the effects of a de-coupling of sex and reproduction (e.g. Bauman, 2003; Beck and Beck-Gernsheim, 1995; Evans, 2004; Giddens, 1992; Luhmann, 1998). This emergent body of popular and academic knowledge about love reflects the growing significance of emotional and intimate life as a domain for defining and governing relations between the sexes. While it is not possible to do justice to this diverse body of research and writing, in line with work on other aspects of the emotions (see Chapters 1 and 2), across disciplines, one can identify broad contending discourses on romantic love focusing on, on the one hand, the biological approach and, on the other, the social constructionist approach. These approaches reflect different assumptions about the self and individual agency, and utilize on different languages and metaphors.

In brief, the biological approach is based on the premise that love is timeless and universal (i.e. unaffected by society), and is therefore adaptive. Referring to evidence from studies of animals and other cultures, proponents of the biological approach view differences between men and women in matters of love as rooted in 'nature'. Love flows from our genes, as part of our evolutionary heritage (Hendrick and Hendrick, 1992: 6). Within this perspective, love is seen as a category of *acts*. As with biological theories of aggression (Chapter 2), the meaning or significance of acts is attributed in a post hoc way. The explanation is derived from the outcome; viz., successful reproduction. This perspective ascribes little autonomy and agency to the self and attaches little significance to the meaning making that occurs in human interaction. Men and women are 'naturally' attracted to each other, much like opposites poles of a magnet, and exercise little control over the power of attraction. However, men and women are constructed differently within this discourse. Men are viewed as genetically 'programmed', or hormonally impelled to be the initiators in sexual encounters, and to be driven by the biological imperatives of reproduction and competition for females (see, e.g. Fausto-Stirling, 1992; Oudshoorn, 1994). Anthropomorphism can be seen in descriptions of evidence taken from the animal world. Writers speak of 'love' in monkeys, as though a concept with such a rich and value-laden history could apply without difficulty to non-human species. This relies on reading meaning into certain animal acts; for example, a baby's close contact with its mother has been described as 'cuddling' and 'caressing', and competition between males over females has been described as 'jealousy' (e.g. Harlow, 1974, cited in Hendrick and Hendrick, pp. 6–9). The limitations of the biological perspective were referred to earlier (see Chapter 2), but include the failure to address issues of power relations and the ten-dency to take existing social arrangements as given. If differences are natural, the argument goes, there is little point trying to change the status quo, since this would be 'against nature'. If men rape in war, or abuse their partners, this is seen as an inevitable product of their reproductive 'hard-wiring'.

Social constructionists, on the other hand, argue that love is a historically variable and 'learnt' phenomenon, and is culturally trans-mitted from one generation to the next by examples, stories, imitation, and direct instruction (Hendrick and Hendrick, 1992: 6–15). Love is an *accomplishment* that presupposes interacting persons, and its endurance depends upon reiterative practices and performances. To experience love, one must *possess* or *be* a 'self' (Hendrick and Hendrick, 1992: 15). The question of whether a particular concept of self is a precondition for the modern notion of romantic love has been a subject of some debate in the literature. However, a strong argument has been made that romantic love could not exist before humans developed a strong sense of individuality or self (see Hendrick and Hendrick, 1992: 21). Rotundo (1993), for example, argues,

> To understand the historical emergence of modern love, we need to understand the appearance of what some have called the 'romantic self'. This is the belief that every person has a unique essence, a fundamental core that remains when all social roles and conventions are stripped away. A man or a woman in love shares that essence with his or her beloved as with no other person. This sharing of one's innermost self is vital to modern romantic love. (Rotundo, 1993: 110)

The notion of the self-contained individual suggests the existence of large areas of opaqueness if the individual chooses not to fully disclose their desires and wishes (Hendrick and Hendrick, 1992: 21–22). The distinction between the 'inner self' or 'private self' and the 'outer self' or 'public self', drawn by some sociologists and social psychologists, suggests that there are aspects of one's experience that the individual 'keeps to themselves' and are separate from that which is open to public presentation. This implies the existence of a high degree of individual autonomy and reflexivity. It should be noted that this is a historically specific concept of self that is not shared by all cultures (Morris, 1994). One common view is that love depends on mutual self-disclosure, which makes one vulnerable to the power of the other. Mutual disclosures between couples who have 'fallen in love' involve a merging of their inner selves so that, in time, the separate selves become one corporate entity conventionally known as 'we'. The notion of 'falling in love' suggests an overwhelming attraction and 'loss of self'. In other words, romantic love could not exist without a strong sense of self to begin with and the mutual disclosure of what is private, particularly about the body. Hence, lovers' desires to mutually explore the body of the other (i.e. 'sex') can be understood as an attempt to know each others' private sensations (Hendrick and Hendrick, 1992: 22). With a growing emphasis on lovers attaining a complete and shared understanding of each other in the nineteenth century, candour began to be accorded an extremely high value. Candour united people who otherwise inhabited separated spheres and allowed them to open up their 'true selves' to the other, to create intimacy and oneness (Rotundo, 1993: 111). Many feminists and masculinity scholars believe that these norms of romantic love work to the disadvantage of women, in that the gender division of emotion in the sphere of love and intimacy results in women doing most of the 'emotion work' (see, e.g. Duncombe and Marsden, 1993). Much critical academic, particularly feminist, work has been oriented to the political task of unsettling taken-for-granted links between love, intimacy, and sex, showing them to reflect and reinforce gender inequalities and heterosexist biases.

Recent constructionist work has sought to uncover the origins of the concept of romantic love, including specifically its biological meanings and associations, with the more critical contributions, mainly from feminist and gay historians, oriented to showing how the language of love has reinforced 'hetero-normative' socio-sexual arrangements (see, e.g. Richardson, 1996). As this work has shown, the notion of romantic love, with its connotations of sexual attraction, and over-whelming desire, is a relatively recent 'invention', dating from as recent as the late eighteenth century, and is by no means universal today. Many Japanese, for example, feel uncomfortable with such declarations as 'I love you', which have come into their language only through the contact with the Romantic literature of the West (Morsbach and Tyler, 1986: 301). In ancient Greece, many people believed that 'true love' was that which occurred between an adult man and an adolescent boy. Passion and intimacy were directed towards these adolescent males more often than towards wives, 'a fact not well explained by evolutionary theories' (Sternberg, 1999: 62).

The notions of 'falling in love' and 'making love', which suggest a union of male and female souls and bodies, respectively, emerged during an age increasingly dominated by the 'two-sex' model and when the passions and imagination began to be valued more highly than other human attributes (Solomon, 1993: 55). According to Luhmann, the Romantic period gave rise to the notion of *passionate* love as the principle upon which the *choice* of a spouse should be based (1998: 129). This focus on passionate love represented a break from the earlier conjugal love, which was based on the model of 'Man's' relationship to God, and focused on preservation of property relations and reproducing one and the same family. That is, what was viewed as important was not living out one's own passions, but rather developing a solidarity within a given order (Hendrick and Hendrick, 1992: 130). Under Romanticism, however, love was endowed with permanence, and became the sole legitimate reason for the choice of a partner. Hence, arranged marriages were replaced by 'marriages of the heart'. As Langford notes, in modern Western societies, marriage and family life have increasingly come to be *based upon* the experience of 'falling in love' (Langford, 1999: 16). A focus on the predetermined and orderly was replaced by an emphasis on the significance of *irrational* forces, both in the universe and in man. Because love is accorded such power, it *appears* to come from *outside the social* (1999: 17). It is interesting to note the development in the meaning of 'passion' under Romanticism. Whereas, 'passion' originally referred to suffering (as in 'the Passion of Christ'), under Romanticism, its meaning expanded considerably, to refer to something that *happens to us*, that renders us passive, such that we *suffer* the happy passions of joy and love, as well as the painful passions of grief, guilt, and despair (Solomon, 1993: 67). As Luhmann argues, one obtains a clearer picture of the change in the semantics of romantic love if one charts changes in the declarations of love. While in the seventeenth century, a declaration of love, to be convincing, needed proof that the lover was a prince or a suitor of the same rank as the lover, by the nineteenth century this was replaced by the declaration of one's intention to marry (Luhmann, 1998: 148). Luhmann also notes that the focus on love under Romanticism did not mean that love was 'democratised' in the sense that it was a capacity available to everyone. 'Loving with "Romantic irony" was not intended for labourers or servant girls'; the Romantic ideal was 'highly selective in terms of the attitudes it presupposed' (1998: 139). Nevertheless, in time, romantic love became the governing ideal for men and women regardless of their social strata, and was seen to provide the basis for a stable, fulfilling marriage.

Some scholars argue that the development of the concept of love during the romantic period went hand in hand with the formation of the *reflexive* kind of self. Romantic literature focused on the concreteness and uniqueness of the individual as a reflexive being. More and more, emphasis was placed on the capacity for, and the enjoyable nature of *feeling* and to suffer because of feeling. A corresponding feeling in the other had to be emotionally affirmed and sought after. 'Love was aimed at an I and a you, to the extent that both were part of the love relationship – i.e. that each made it possible for the other to have such a relationship – and not because both were good, or beautiful, or noble or rich.' (Luhmann, 1998: 138). As Giddens observes, 'romantic love presupposes some degree of self-interrogation. How do I feel about the other? How does the other feel about me? Are our feelings "profound" enough to support a long-term involvement?' (1992: 44). Romantic love was a feminised love, in that women were ascribed primary responsibility for fostering love. That is, ideas about love were allied to women's subordination in the home and their separation from the public sphere (Giddens, 1992: 43). It involved 'the quest' in that validation of the self awaited the discovery of the other. Romantic love has an active character, which is shown in romance novels; 'the heroin meets and melts the heart of a man who is initially indifferent to and aloof from her, or openly hostile'

(1992: 46). Although often portrayed in literature and everyday life as the means whereby a woman meets 'Mr Right', the ethos of romantic love involves 'a process of the creation of a mutual narrative biography'. 'The heroine tames, softens and alters the seemingly intractable masculinity of her love object, making it possible for mutual affection to become the main guiding-line of their lives together' (Giddens, 1992: 46).

Sexuality has been a recurring theme in the discourses of romantic love and, indeed, it may be said that it is 'the condition for both the survival and enhancement of love' (Luhmann, 1998: 148). By becoming involved in close, 'intimate' relationships, and especially sexually based relationships, the individual seeks certainties that will go beyond the moment. Love was no longer exclusively dependent on the demonstration of physical and moral qualities, which was a feature of earlier courtly love. As Hendrick and Hendrick (1992) note, the Romantic focus on love was such that it sometimes seemed objectless. Whereas in the Middle Ages religious thinking developed the idea of 'God is love', Romanticism evolved the philosophy that 'love is God', and also developed the concept of sexual love as an ideal that could provide the basis for fulfilment for all men and women (Hendrick and Hendrick, 1992: 39). However, the more emphasis was placed on the individual and on personal fulfilment, 'the more improbable it became that one would encounter partners *possessing the characteristics expected*' (Luhmann, 1982: 134; emphasis in original). Consequently, the theme of unrequited love has been a feature of the discourse of romantic love.

The idea that romantic love is a passionate force, and an over-whelming attraction for the other, can be seen in the recent literature on the psychology of emotions. In their widely cited psychology text, *Love, Sex and Intimacy*, Hatfield and Rapson (1993), for example, describe passionate love as 'a "hot", intense emotion' that is 'some-times labeled obsessive love, puppy love, a crush, lovesickness, infatuation, or being-in-love'. They define it as,

A state of intense longing for union with another. Passionate love is a complex functional whole including appraisals or appreciations, subjective feelings, expressions, patterned physiological processes, action tendencies, and instrumental behaviours. Reciprocated love (union with the other) is associated with fulfilment and ecstasy; unrequited love (separation) with emptiness, anxiety, or despair. (Hatfield and Rapson, 1993: 5)

As the above description and definition suggests, passionate love has come to be seen as including both rational and irrational components and to involve a complex set of bio-psycho-social responses. The description of passionate love as 'a "hot" intense emotion' conveys its physical hold over us, while terms such as 'obsessive', 'puppy love' and 'lovesickness' suggest a feeling that is beyond the control of the rational human mind. Increasingly, in psychology, love is seen to encompass elements that can be teased apart and categorised and as subject to systematic study and evaluation; for example, the intensity of feeling can be likened to heat or warmth, and to involve different degrees of attachment or commitment to the other. Hatfield and Rapson, along with other psychologists, have in particular sought to distinguish compassionate love from 'companionate love' (alternatively 'true love' or 'conjugal love'), which they say is a '"warm", far less intense emotion' (1993: 8). This latter kind of love, they say, 'combines feelings of deep attachment, commitment, and intimacy' (1993: 8).

Psychologists have developed a number of scales for measuring the various components of 'passionate love', and for categorising 'love styles', suggesting that love can be understood objectively and ahistorically. For example, Sternberg (1986) has developed a 'love taxonomy', involving 'seven kinds of love', based on the presence or absence of the three components of intimacy, passion, and decision/ commitment (see Cramer, 1998: 153–154), while Hatfield and Sprecher (1986) designed the Passionate Love Scale, to tap the cognitive, emotional, and behavioural components of 'longing for union' (see Hatfield and Rapson, 1993: 6–8). Hatfield and Rapson cite evidence from a study of Caucasian, Filipino, and Japanese men and women showing that, on average, men and women from these ethnic groups seemed to love with equal passion (1993: 6). The effort to apply such a scale cross-culturally reveals the belief that 'love' exists as an objective category, independent of context and of the diverse meanings attributed to it and that the primary task of social science is to find adequate methods to uncover its 'essence'. This governing ideal of love has informed explanations of men's and women's actions, in particular its power over that which is rational, and has arguably played a considerable role in defining and regulating relations between men and women.

The idea that love has a power of its own, such that it can induce a kind of madness in the affected, and indeed 'drive' one to crime, is reflected in the notion of *crime passionnel* ('crime of passion'). One dictionary definition of a crime of passion is 'a crime committed under the influence of passionate feelings, usually feelings of sexual jealousy' (Editorial Staff, 1981: 443). This suggests that, like those 'under the influence' of a powerful drug, the perpetrator of the crime of the passion is somehow not fully responsible for their actions which should therefore be excused. Interestingly, although this term is not specific to gender or sexual preference, it has a strong masculine connotation and tends to be applied to cases of male-to-female abuse or murder in heterosexual monogamous relationships. For instance, in a recent and highly publicised murder case in France, in which a rock star Bertrand Cantat killed his partner, Marie Trintignant, a famous actress, it was suggested that Cantat was 'driven' by a 'crime of passion'. It was reported in the news media that prior to the murder, 'the couple were absorbed in each other, shutting out friends and colleagues' (Vulliamy, 2003: 31). Trintignant was described as having had a series of 'highly charged' relationships prior to her relationship with Cantat, and 'like her heroines ... was a woman who often failed to master her own strong emotions'. (The reference here to 'often failed to master her own emotions' reveals a distinctly feminine weakness: masculinity is defined by the ability to control the emotions.) She was portrayed as a vulnerable individual desperately searching for 'true love', who was ironically and sadly turned against by her lover during a crazed attack. Cantat was claimed to have said that love 'is a tango space in which one dances with one's demons ... Love exists in a shell and there is something terrible within it ... I need to reduce love to something liveable with'. One writer described the affair as 'love to the limits, between a femme fatale and a great but trapped man – seekers of the absolute, they shared the poetry of passion', while *Paris Match* compared the couple to Romeo and Juliet (Vulliamy, 2003: 33). Women's groups, on the other hand, seized on the killing to denounce 'everything in our culture which hides this crime' and to call on battered women to 'come forward, dare to speak out' (Vulliamy, 2003: 31). The idea that love exerts a 'power over' the individual serves to excuse men from the violence done to women, who are usually the victims of such 'irrational' outbursts.

Challenges to, and changes in conceptions of 'passionate' or 'romantic' love

Although the notion of 'passionate' or 'romantic love' has become pervasive in the modern Western world as the love that defines intimate relations between the sexes, it has by no means remained unchallenged or been unchanging through its history. A major challenge to the ideal of romantic love was offered by many women and liberal reformers in the second half of the nineteenth century. The growing economic independence of women led them to demand emotional fulfilment rather than economic security in marriage, and to challenge the romantic ideals that underpinned marriage and worked to their disadvantage. Newspaper articles, novels, plays, public speeches and private conversations centred on the New Woman – a term invented in 1894 to describe what was by then a familiar phenomenon (Yalom, 2001: 268). Debates about 'The Woman Question' raged throughout Europe, raising awareness about the privileges enjoyed by men, with many women demanding for a more egalitarian relationship between spouses or the rejection of marriage altogether (Yalom, 2001: 263–279). In the US also, during the late nineteenth and early twentieth centuries, many women sought greater autonomy for themselves with and without marriage, while many commentators expressed concern that the institution of marriage was in major crisis (Illouz, 1997; Yalom, 2001: 280–293). Newspaper and magazine columnists, among others, criticised the emerging mass culture for instilling the new ideal of romance as a purely 'fictional' or cinematic entity. At the same time, diverse experts, including lawyers, psychologists, and sociologists, invoked alternative models of a good marriage: 'marriage as friendship, marriage as a partnership or companionship, marriage as a contract, marriage as a skilful art, and marriage as requiring effort' (Illouz, 1997: 51).

The idea that a lasting marriage required 'hard work', and that boredom can kill love, began to gain credence among the public in the first decades of the twentieth century. In discussions about the basis for a 'workable' marriage, the idea of 'uncontrolled' drives of romance and passion was exchanged for the 'controlled management' of one's emotions. There was a concern to find 'a more reliable basis for love than romantic passion without losing love itself in the process' (Illouz, 1997: 52). As Illouz notes, 'fun' and 'work' were accommodated in the 'modern, hybrid romantic ethos'. Keeping passion alive required constant 'hard work'.

> To be successful, a couple now had to combine spontaneity and calculation, the ability to negotiate with a taste for 'hot romance'. The hedonistic therapeutic model that emerged was characterized by such phrases as 'having a good time together', 'sharing common interests', 'talking', 'getting to know each other', 'understanding the other person's needs', and 'compromising'. (Illouz, 1997: 53)

Illouz links the emergence of this new hybrid ethos to the growing 'commodification of romance'. That is, evolving conceptions of intimacy and sexuality were bound up with the new business of leisure and technologies of leisure, such as the automobile and movie theatre (1997: 54). By the turn of the century, the courtship practice of 'calling', which took place within the private and protected space of the family and home was gradually replaced by 'dating', whereby couples would 'go out' to leisure pursuits (1997: 55). Recently, the commodification of romance has been elevated to new levels, with a host of new practices and industries focusing on dating and sexual pleasure. There are many examples of this, some of which will be reviewed in the paragraphs which follow. However, perhaps the clearest example is the flourishing dating industry, seen in new television shows, such as ITV1's *Love on a Saturday Night*, and BB2's *Would Like to Meet*, in the UK. The Internet has opened an array of new possibilities for dating, by allowing one to examine the 'profiles' of potential partners/lovers – referred to in the excerpt at the beginning of this chapter. 'Speed dating' has also become increasing popular in recent years. The question is, do such practices disrupt conventional notions of romantic love as portrayed above; that is, a mutual attraction followed by a process of 'falling in love' between opposite sexes? And, do they signal a change in gender norms and relations, with a reduction of differences in expectations concerning men's and women's behaviours?

Online dating and 'speed dating'

On the face of it, online dating and 'speed dating' would seem to challenge some traditional norms governing the development of intimate relations between the sexes, particularly as regards men and women playing prescribed, complementary roles and of couples gradually 'getting to know each other' over an extended period of time. According to Deyo and Deyo, in their book, *Speed Dating: The Smarter, Faster Way to Lasting Love* (2002), speed dating originated in Los Angeles, after a series of meetings they organised with their students in order to 'discuss ways to address Jewish intermarriage', but quickly grew to 'weekly events in twenty-five cities worldwide' (2002: xv–xvi). That is, the practice seems to have its origins with a fairly conventional concern with controlling mate selection within a cultural group, with the help of third-party intermediaries. This form of dating, which calls on potential lovers to make a selection within a delimited period of time (Deyo and Deyo stipulate seven minutes, though some advertised services indicate less) is seen to allow couples (assumed to be heterosexual) to 'quickly and more confidently assess a relationship' (2002: xiv). The phenomenon involves groups of men and women (each with a name tag and a scorecard) meeting at a central location (e.g. café), then being paired off at tables for two for a limited period to get acquainted with each other. Internet sites, of which there are a substantial number, provide those potentially interested in participating in 'speed dating' with details of what will be required of them should they choose to participate. In brief, after the designated period, a bell rings, and the couple mark on their card whether or not they would have an interest in meeting their date again, and then move on to the next table. If a mutual interest is noted, the organizers of the 'event' provide each party with the other's phone number (see http://health.discovery.com/centres/loverelationships/articles/speed_dating.html; http://www.xdate.co.uk/index.asp). According to websites, these services are oriented to 'busy' single people who do not have the time for other ways of meeting others (bars, blind dates, dating services, online, etc.), and who want more control over the choice of a potential companion. One site, XDating, summarises the advantages of 'speed dating': 'rejection free; check for chemistry first; meet 25 potential partners in one place; a fun night out; no enduring tedious blind dates; high success rate; a self-confidence

booster; and good therapy for shyness' (http://www.xdate.co.uk/
index.asp). Advertised at one website as a 'facilitated introduction',
'speed dating' is recommended for 'people who aren't comfortable
with, or just tired of, many of the traditional dating approaches'
(http://www.pre-dating.com). As a number of websites explain, this
apparently 'unconventional' arrangement has a 'conventional' basis –
'simply chemistry' (http://health.discovery.com/centres/loverelation-
ships/articles/speed_dating.html). In other words, 'speed dating' is seen
to simply facilitate the natural process by which people are naturally
drawn together, by saving time and offering more choice in the
selection of potential partners, and as such does not offer a challenge
to the ideals of romantic love. There is no questioning of that which
is presumed to be a universally expressed desire (passionate love and,
ultimately, marriage).

In recent years, online dating has also become a popular phenomenon of global dimensions. Some online dating agencies have had
great commercial success, with companies such as Match.com having a database in the order of millions, and employing increasingly
sophisticated means of profiling members in order to bring about the
best possible match (Orr, 2004: 148–149). Text-messaging is among
the services offered by some companies, with a number (e.g. SMS.ac)
allowing people to send and receive messages from their mobile
phones and other wireless devices in order to arrange dates or to flirt
(Orr, 2004: 152). Some Sky services (Koopid and Dateline) allow
digital viewers to find matches from a data set and then communicate with other members of the service via voicemail, post or TV
email (Dubberley, 2004: 26). The purported advantage of online dating is the ability to screen potential mates over the Internet before
meeting so as to avoid wasting time with unsuitable matches, and to
protect the searchers' anonymity and security. The screening and
security aspect would seem to be an especially positive development
for women who tend to be more vulnerable to sexual exploitation
and unwanted attention. Some services take speed dating online
(e.g. Love Puzzle.co.uk), but allow people greater choice before the
event. That is, singles register online and identify those who they
would like to date. Users' choices are then cross-referenced and only
dates requested by both parties feature on the agenda. (Partners are
provided with an agenda of 15-minute dates for the evening

[Dubberley, 2004: 27].) There is no doubt that new media technologies, used singly and in combination, are providing new avenues for people to connect and to relate.

The global spread of speed dating and online dating in recent years is an interesting sociological phenomenon. The fact that they have been taken up in many cultures suggests that they address a widespread need and perhaps dissatisfaction with more traditional haphazard, 'hit-and-miss', and time-consuming approaches, for example, meeting in public bars. They purportedly allow women and men to 'cast a wider net' than more traditional methods, and to be more 'targeted' in their search for love. A positive interpretation of the practices is that they are a democratising force, providing people with more choice and control, allowing busy professionals to find a better balance between their work and social lives, and equalising the balance between men and women in the process of partner choice and the development of intimate and loving relationships (see, e.g. Dubberley, 2004: 26). One writer, Ben-Ze'ev, the author of *Love Online: Emotions on the Internet* (2004), suggests that online relationships are egalitarian since external appearance and other characteristics can be disregarded. This has particularly advantaged women whose external appearances generally have more weight in men's judgement of women than in women's judgement of men (Ben-Ze'ev, 2004: 109, 160, 178–179). More profoundly, Ben-Ze'ev argues,

> The Internet has dramatically changed the romantic domain; this process will accelerate in the future. Such changes will inevitably modify present social forms such as marriage and cohabitation, and current romantic practices relating to courtship, casual sex, committed romantic relationships, and romantic exclusivity. (2004: 247)

On the other hand, there is evidence to suggest that this way of developing new relationships presents a number of problems for users, including an over-abundance of choice (which proves time consuming rather than time saving), deception behind anonymity, inflated expectations of finding the 'right' partner, mismatched motives (e.g. love versus extorting money), and the difficulty of discriminating among people with similar profiles (Orr, 2004: 98, 151–163). Some commentators believe that online dating services facilitate infidelity (by making discrete connection relatively risk free) and encourage those who are looking for easy sex rather than a romantic encounter (Orr, 2004: 127–136, 155). While some internet users report an 'emotionally purer' (i.e. less embodied) 'love' and more active and intense sex online – in some cases better than actual 'offline sex' (see Ben-Ze'ev, 2004) – there is much scope for deception, which may not be the best basis for 'love' (Mullan, 2004: 13). As Orr indicates, some services have drawn on sexual and cultural stereotypes to promote their services, for example by sending out spam mailings with messages like: 'Tired of dating spoiled American women? Russian women are unspoiled, devoted and grateful' (Orr, 2004: 96). The view promoted by some online dating services, such as Match.com, that online dating is simply addressing a *universal* need – the desire for love – denies the cultural specific character of views on dating and love (see, e.g. Overing and Passes, 2000). It also denies the fact that service providers sometimes see poorer countries as simply another way for men in rich countries to expand their pool of options by exploiting women who are sometimes desperate to escape oppressive conditions (Orr, 2004: 96–102). Further, the view that online dating is democratising denies the vastly unequal access to the Internet in the West and in many of the countries where services are being increasingly targeted; for example, India, Columbia, Russia (Orr, 2004: 93–98).

Changing discourses of sexuality and gender

According to some sociologists, recent changes in the conduct of sexual relationships, including the norms of dating, such as those described, reflect a loosening of the connections between sexuality, reproduction, and marriage, and a closing of the gap in gender differences in sexual desire and sexual conduct. Giddens (1992) sees an increasing freeing of sexuality from reproduction, kinship, and generations, to create what he calls 'plastic sexuality' which he believes leads – in principle – to a lessening of the 'overweening importance of male sexual experience'. This new form of sexuality, he argues, was 'a precondition for the sexual revolution of the past several decades' and has resulted in a 'revolution in female sexual autonomy' with profound consequences for male sexuality (Giddens, 1992: 2, 27–28). In Giddens' view, this form of sexuality provides the foundation for a 'pure relationship', a union of sexual and emotional equality, whereby interactions can be initiated for their own sake and which is continued only insofar as both parties derive enough satisfactions from it (1992: 58). The pure relationship, Giddens contends, is part of a 'generic restructuring of intimacy' that emerges in other contexts of sexuality besides heterosexual marriage and is bound up with broader developments in modernity and social changes in the last few decades. The concept of the 'pure relationship' can be criticised for being idealistic in denying the relations of power in all relationships (including ones that are relatively economically equal) and the continuing salience of 'marriage', both as a discourse shaping the conception and expression of romantic love and as an institution governing socio-sexual arrangements. Recent debates surrounding homosexual marriage, and its continuing illegality in many juris-dictions, have underlined the continuing significance of marriage as an institution for the expression of *opposite* sex love (see, e.g. Connolly, 2001; Younge, 2003).

More recently, Beck and Beck-Gernsheim (1995) have also documented the changing nature of love in conjunction with sexual relations and family forms in late modern society. The erosion of traditional society and of the strict rules and regulations as to how to behave, they argue, has created greater potential for choice and 'more possibilities to choose from' in intimate life and more generally. The weakening of rigid gender roles, which provided the basis for industrial society, combined with increasing individualisation and uncertainty about how people should conduct their lives, has lead to a search for new forms of identity, stability, and fulfilment. In this context, love acquires heightened significance, for providing 'emotional and mental stability', and people demand more than in the past from those they love. The common ground in marriage is 'almost exclusively emotional', without which the marriage cannot endure. As Beck and Beck-Gernsheim argue, this situation has generated an ever-present tension between 'being yourself and being part of a lasting togetherness with someone who is equally in search of his/her own self' (Beck and Beck-Gernsheim, 1995: 77).

Although Giddens' and Beck and Beck-Gernsheim's accounts differ in a number of respects, they share the view that the ideals and norms of love, sex, and intimacy, and gender roles, are changing as a result of the changing conditions of late modern society and especially the process of individualisation. More and more individuals are freed from social constraints and the rigidities of prescribed social roles, so that they are able to choose among a vast variety of lifestyle options, to create their identities – a process which generates new opportunities and freedoms but also growing demands on, and tensions within, intimate relationships. On the face of it, there seems to be much in this argument, and so it is worth examining the evidence in some detail. Innovations such as speed dating and online dating suggest that women like men are confronted with more 'choice', and are more likely than in the past to demand sexual satisfaction outside a loving relationship and marriage, to choose to have extra-marital affairs, and to initiate sexual encounters. Such 'choice' would appear to challenge the norms of romantic love and monogamous hetero-sexuality as they have developed in the West. An increasing media focus on women's sex lives and relationships suggests that sex roles have changed or are changing, and that there is greater scope for women's engagement in practices not tolerated in the past, in the West at least. Television serials, such as *Sex and the City*, the ready availability of porn via cable TV and Internet, and increasing explicitness in sexual scenes in movies generally, may be taken as indicators of these changing norms and practices, and perhaps growing gender equality. The excerpt at the beginning of this chapter, which is directed at a female readership, is but one example of what may be argued to be an example of changes in gender roles and of the links between traditional prescriptive gender roles and views on, and orientations to sex. At the same time, debate about traditional gender roles within the family, including the negotiation of sexual encounters, gained pace in the 1990s. The steady increase in the percentage of families with the dual-earner couple in much of the West has undoubtedly been one factor contributing to this debate (see Yalom, 2001: 379–391). Working women have asked how men may play a more prominent role in the domestic sphere, by undertaking more of the 'emotional work' of caring and fathering and thereby share the burden of the 'double shift' that has been the working woman's lot.

A recent scholarly interest in the social constructions and stereo-types of fatherhood, and how these serve to limit men's involvement with their children and to preserve gender inequality, can be taken as one indication of this new sensibility about men's involvement in domestic life (see, e.g. LaRossa, 1997; Marsiglio, 1995), although some see this as a way of asserting the importance of the traditional, that is, male-headed, heterosexual nuclear family (see, e.g. Segal, 1990: 53).

Women's magazines have also reflected shifts in women's domestic role. For example, magazines such as *Good Housekeeping, Family Circle, Woman's Day*, and *Better Homes and Gardens* that were 'originally oriented to traditional wives with children' are today 'claiming the sexually explicit content that used to be the exclusive purview of magazines intended for single women (e.g. *Glamour, Cosmopolitan*, and *Mademoiselle*)' (Yalom, 2001: 392). However, notwithstanding these developments, it needs to be asked just how far constructions of gender have changed over recent decades in the West. Have the power relations of gender altered such that men and women can enter and conduct relationships on equal terms? Is there any evidence that the sexual practices of men and women have altered significantly?

The media in its diverse forms, including news media (print and broadcast), the Internet, wide-circulation magazines, and other popular writings, provides one barometer of change in relation to sexual norms, although they offer limited insight into the actual practices that are reported and portrayed. Recent news reports certainly suggest increasing 'liberalisation' in regard to sexual matters, particularly as they pertain to women. One recent article, for example, reports women's apparent eagerness to use a website (Casual Encounters of Craiglist.com) which is for 'people who want "one-off, no ties, no nonsense sex"'. It noted that in the six months since the website was launched in London (http://london.craiglist.org), the Casual Encounters page had had 280,000 hits, with around 42,000 of them from women – 'an unusually high proportion'. (No evidence is provided of what would be considered a 'usual' proportion.) One commentator, 'a psychotherapist for *Cosmopolitan* magazine', is quoted: 'I've been worried about soulless sex imposed on women by the ladette culture but the fact that this site is so popular proves that hardcore, testosterone-driven sex is genuinely what some women really want.' The article cites the case of one woman who used the site. She was quoted: 'I'd been single for eight months and although what I really wanted was a boyfriend, it the meantime I was sexually frustrated and desperate for physical affection.' The article goes on to note that the woman, 'a 31-year-old IT specialist from northern London', had met three men through the site in the preceding six months. As she explained:

> I get the men to send me their pictures but don't give them mine, which means they don't recognise me when we meet, giving me

the opportunity of changing my mind even at the last minute ...
The first man I met was so handsome we didn't even finish our
drinks before heading back to my flat. It was so exciting. I felt
amazingly liberated because we were both clear and honest about
what we wanted. When he left the next morning I didn't mind at
all and am completely happy that we haven't been in contact
since. (Hill, 2003: 7)

These comments may be taken to indicate that the norms around
sexual liaisons may be changing and that women who use the
technology of the Internet are exerting a greater control over choice
of partners and sexual practices than was possible for women in the
past. However, the article offers no analysis of why women may use
these sites, what they expect from them, and how common their use is
relative to other, more traditional methods of contact. Interestingly,
the article concludes by noting that the above woman 'refused to
take the second man she met back home because she thought there
was something odd about him, and was left disillusioned by the
third man', and that she had come to realise that 'it's not just sex
I want: it is a real relationship'. As she was quoted: 'I don't think
I'll be using the site again; it just left me feeling sadder and lonelier
than before' (Hill, 2003: 7). This hints that, at least for some women,
there may be more involved in the use of such sites than the desire
for an unattached sexual liaison.

Other evidence from recent news media also lends the impression
that there is growing equalisation between women and men as regards
concerns for sexual satisfaction. For example, a series of articles
appearing in UK newspapers in 2002 and 2003 announced research and
new medical treatments for a number of female sexual 'conditions',
such as 'general lack of desire' and 'female sexual dysfunction'. One
article, published in *The Observer*, notes that scientists had 'successfully
tested a nasal spray, PT-141, that sent "healthy, normal women" into
states of high sexual arousal', and that a company hopes to market
the spray to humans 'in two or three years', and particularly to 'men
with impotence and women with low arousal' (McKie, 2002: 1).
Another article, again in *The Observer*, reported that 'Women suffering
sexual problems ranging from general lack of desire to severe genital
deformity are being prescribed vibrators on the National Health Service
to help them rediscover their sex drive.' The article reports that some

doctors have begun referring patients with sexual dysfunction to sex shops 'for advice on exploring their bodies' (one consultant in sexual dysfunction was quoted that 'Almost half of all women suffer from a sexual dysfunction') and that some had bought vibrators for their practices (Hill, 2002). And, more recently, in the business pages of *The Independent*, it was reported that a clitoral stimulator made of PVC, 'launched in Boots earlier this year' was 'currently selling 3,500 boxes a week at £9.99 apiece', and was to be made 'available at other chemists from the New Year'. The article noted that 'The company believes sexual dysfunction, which according to a 1999 study published in the *Journal of American Medical Association* affects up to 43 per cent of adult women, could eventually rival the $4 billion market for male erectile dysfunction products such as Viagra' (Foley, 2003: 18). However, again, although there appears to be greater latitude than in the past for discussion about sexual matters in general, and about women's sexual satisfaction in particular, it is not clear that norms governing gender relations have changed to a significant extent.

The impact of consumerism

Rather than reflecting a substantial change in gender roles and relations, such media portrayals can be viewed, rather, as evidence of the pervasive impact of consumerism and market rationality on everyday, including intimate, life (see, e.g. Hochschild, 2003). More and more, market relations and globalising influences have infiltrated personal life, so that we have begun to view our love lives and intimate relationships in terms of the logic of consumer capitalism. In her analysis of best selling advice books for women published in the US in the late twentieth century, Hochschild (2003) notes how such books recycle the male rules of love. They assert that 'it's a "feminine" practice to subordinate the importance of love, to delay falling in love until after consolidating a career, to separate love from sex, and for married women to have occasional affairs' (2003: 27). As Hochschild concludes from her analysis, 'We've moved from living according to two emotional codes – one for men and one for women – to a unisex code based on the old code for men' (Hochschild, 2003: 27). Also, it can be argued that, as with men, women are seen as entitled to sexual fulfilment through having access to the market, which extends to the treatment of sexual 'dysfunctions'. Clearly, the pharmaceutical industry has much to gain from the medicalisation of women's sexuality and from the promotion of the idea that supposed sexual problems can be solved through the consumption of certain treatments. Much as Viagra has been a boon for a pharmaceutical industry focusing on men's impotence, clitoral stimulators and other similar gadgets for women promise great profits for their manufacturers. In matters of love and sex, fulfilment and 'freedom' are believed to come through the exercise of individual choice and having the ability to control one's future by 'correct' planning, management, and purchasing decisions. This can be seen in the language and arguments of a number of recent advice books devoted to dating and finding sexual partners. Such books, which make liberal use of terms such as 'empowerment' and 'efficiency', assume a particular conception of self: one keen to undertake intense work on the self, to become 'smarter', more efficient, and more in touch with one's desires and needs. One is expected to conduct one's love life as an entrepreneur; that is, be calculating and strategically minded, with an eye to opportunities and risks. It is worth looking closely at some recent examples of these books, since they illustrate how deeply the logic and language of the market and of rational planning have infiltrated matters of the heart.

Deyo and Deyo's book, *Speed Dating*, referred to above, insists that success in dating is to 'date smarter, not longer' (mimicking the adage 'Work smarter, not harder'). By adopting the suggested methods, it is claimed, singles have 'escap[ed] the pain and confusion of trad- itional dating' and 'achieve[ed] empowerment and clarity' (Deyo and Deyo, 2002: xv). Readers are presented with a series of 'SpeedDating Exercises', which encourage them to reflect upon their thoughts, in relation to one's self and one's date. It is an approach underpinned by a belief in the power of introspection: 'if you are being true to yourself, through being honest about your values and goals . . . you stand the best chance of finding your lifelong partner' (Deyo and Deyo, 2002: 170). One exercise invites the reader: 'The next time you are dating someone and believe you might be in love, complete the following checklist to assist you in determining whether it has the potential to last'. The 'checklist' includes items such as 'articulat[e] four (nonphysical) virtues about the person that I respect . . .', and 'As my date discusses her goals and dreams, I feel interested and truly motivated to help her attain them – or at least I can be encouraging' (Deyo and Deyo, 2002: 24). Another exercise instructs: 'Become aware of your thoughts that run through your mind throughout the day. Note what types of thoughts you typically have: Are they positive? Are they negative or destructive? Are they coming from emotion? Are they coming from the intellect?' The reader is instructed that if they have any 'destructive thoughts' they should 'strategize how to address them', such as 'find ways of pushing them out of your mind' and 'consider asking one of your SpeedDating team members to help you'. Further, 'While you're on the date, notice your thoughts in evaluating the date.' 'Are the thoughts coming from your emotions...' 'Are the thoughts coming from your intellect...', 'Are the thoughts and emotions consistent with each other, or opposing?' And, 'Are the thoughts "destructive": "He'll never want to go out with me again because I said that really stupid thing"' (Deyo and Deyo, 2002: 110). The book urges readers to gain a better understanding of what motivates them in relationships, by gaining a better understanding and control of their emotions. It notes that for 'Most people' their emotions 'dominate their thinking, especially when they are involved in a relationship', while for some their 'intellect dominates their emotions, impeding their progress in love'. It contends that 'By realising that desires drive thoughts and thoughts drive actions, you are in a better position to more accurately and quickly evaluate the potential for a relationship to last' (Deyo and Deyo, 2002: 108–109). The book concludes with a 'Soul Mate Checklist' to help the reader 'recognise your soul mate', noting that, 'If you are aware of who you are and what you are looking for, you'll be better prepared to recognize the right person when you meet her.'

Rachel Greenwald's book, *The Program: How to Find a Husband after Thirty* (2004) – a book directed to women over 30 – is strongly informed by business language and thinking. As Greenwald explains, 'The odds of finding a partner change after 30'; however, 'there's no cause for alarm, because in this step you are going to make a crucial shift in looking for Mr Right that will unveil many new eligible men...You are going to cast a wider net' (2004: 59). In her book, Greenwald outlines a '15-step action program to help you find a husband that uses marketing tactics I learned at Harvard Business School and honed in my professional marketing career' (2004: 3). It goes on to say that 'You, the reader, are the "product", and The Program is a "strategic plan" to help you "market" yourself to find a future partner'. The steps in the strategic plan include 'developing a market focus' ('focus' meaning a 'single-minded dedication to the exclusion of all else'), finding 'marketing support' (a program mentor), 'packaging' ('create your best look'), 'market expansion' ('cast a wider net'), 'branding' onself ('what makes you different'), 'advertising' ('promoting your personal brand'), 'telemarketing' ('get out your address book'), a 'quarterly performance review' ('evaluate your results'), and an 'exit strategy' ('"manage" the process of determining whether he *is* the one, and "manage" him towards commitment') (Greenwald, 2004: 233; emphasis in original). Greenwald recommends establishing a 'dedicated budget for finding your partner', and stresses the importance of 'market research', of proper planning, efficiency, and of 'cut[ting] one's losses' and of 'look[ing] for the next opportunity' when things don't work out as planned. In this schema, there is seen to be no essential difference between running a business and establishing a relationship, and if one can adhere to proper principles of planning and management, it is assumed, there is no reason why one cannot satisfy one's desire for a loving relationship. Consistent with this perspective, each of the chapters of the book finish with a 'checklist' of items that need to be mastered before one can move on to the next step. For example, at the end of the chapter, 'Advertising', the reader is instructed that before proceeding with the next chapter ('Online marketing: be efficient') one should have:

1. Achieved a solid comfort level with promoting your personal brand.
2. Created and sent personalised cards in a direct mail campaign to advertise your brand and specifically asked for introductions.
3. Mastered the art of subtle word-of-mouth advertising and promoted your personal brand to ten targeted people over the course of two weeks.
4. Evaluated your image advertising efforts with the consistency checklist in this chapter.
5. Practiced customising your image advertising message on your next date.
6. Passed the brand recall test. (Greenwald, 2004: 96)

This approach reveals a concept of the self as entrepreneur and the expectation that life should be lived as an enterprise that involves investment decisions, strategic plans, marketing strategies, and the calculation of profits and losses. The extensive use of the language of choice, opportunity, and risk management here implies a calculating approach to finding a sexual partner and an instrumental attitude to the other. That there are a burgeoning number of such 'self-help' books addressed to what appears to be an eager singles market indicates how widespread the assumption has become that people have the power to control their own lives and relationships, and can achieve their goals with the 'right' advice. When one closely examines contemporary practices of sex and intimacy, however, it can be seen that the expectations for women continue to be considerably different than for men in these spheres.

Contemporary practices of sex and intimacy

The following exchange recently appeared in *Good Housekeeping*, a basically conservative magazine which was founded in the mid-1880s to keep 'women abreast of the latest fads and fashions', but has through its history reflected changes in gender roles and sexual mores (Yalom, 2001: 286).

He's only interested in sex

Q I feel under enormous pressure from my husband. He's hit middle age and seems to feel sex is the most important thing in life. But I value other things – affection and conversation – and have become less interested in a physical relationship. Please explain to me why this happens to men when they reach middle age – is it the male menopause? And, if so, what can I do about it?

There's no one way to explain the 'male menopause'; what happens to men varies just as it does to women. But you do need to rebuild the bond between you because without that you'll never want to have sex with him again, and he won't want to be emotionally intimate. For a close couple, I'd suggest that trying [sic] to reach a compromise together – a balance of love-making, cuddling and talking. But I sense such pressure from your husband and such distaste from you that I'm not convinced that would work.

Instead I suggest you contact [name of agency] and book some sessions with a counsellor. (Good advice column, *Good Housekeeping*, April 2002, p. 88)

This articulation of a problem of a personal relationship difficulty focusing on sex and intimacy in this way would have been highly improbable three or four decades ago. However, the assumptions about gender differences that underlie this exchange are relatively long standing in modern Western societies. The idea that men are obsessed with and are the instigators of sex while women place a higher value on emotional intimacy and are relatively passive sexually is firmly entrenched in many contemporary societies. Both popular culture and expert literature reinforce the message that men are more easily able to separate sex from intimacy and love than are women. This is seen most clearly in discussions about men's use of prostitutes and pornography. Moreover, the emotional division of labour extends to resolving problems of sex and intimacy: women are expected to take the lead in nurturing relationships and in resolving problems whereas men tend to 'keep their emotions to themselves'. It is difficult to imagine a man writing the above letter about his wife given these taken-for-granted assumptions.

The advice offered above also reveals much about cultural views regarding the 'normal' conduct of intimate relationships and what makes relationships 'work'. That is, without the necessary preliminary bonding, it is assumed, the woman will not want sex and the man will not want to be 'emotionally intimate'. This implies that, for women, emotional intimacy is a necessary condition for sex, and that for men the opposite is the case. This difference in approach to sex and intimacy is widely seen to be the basis for many relationship difficulties and for the frequent failure for the ideal of romantic love, described earlier, to be realised. There are numerous self-help books offering advice on how to re-ignite one's romantic life by promoting a better mutual understanding between the sexes, particularly in relation to sexual communication and practice. The above exchange indicates how partners are expected to deal with problems of intimate relations in contemporary societies: namely, the use of confession, and counselling. Increasingly, we are compelled to share our intimate problems with others, particularly experts and, when problems cannot be resolved within relationships, we are encouraged to follow the therapeutic route. Historical research has revealed that these views about differences between the sexes, about how to nurture relationships, and about how to deal with sexual problems are a relatively recent 'invention', taking shape just a little over one hundred years ago. The idea that sexual fulfilment underpins a loving relationship and that the resolution of sexual problems can solve matters of the heart came into being with sexual science that began to evolve in the late nineteenth century (see Bland and Doan, 1998a, b; Bullough, 1994; Russett, 1989). In the twentieth century, there developed a thriving sexology industry, which made extensive use of the sexual survey (Erickson, 1999). Experts began to promote the view that sex formed the basis of marital relationships, while the new ideology of sex was celebrated in magazines, newspapers, and movies. At the same time, advertising used sexual desire to sell products and sexual freedom as a commodity (Erickson, 1999: 37). As Erickson observes, 'Men began to feel they had a right to sexual happiness rather than a duty to suppress desire' (1999: 37). At the same time, women were being constructed as sexually passive and as the object of men's desire, and as being at the mercy of their internal chemistry. Hormonal women and ageing women, in particular, began to be seen as subject to 'hormonal imbalance', and thus potentially 'out of control' (Vines, 1993: 7).

The work of Havelock Ellis, whose book *Studies in the Psychology of Sex* (1925) explored, among things, differences between men's and women's 'sexual impulses', and how these provided the basis for problems between the sexes, and particularly women's 'frigidity', is indicative of emergent views on sexual difference. Though expressed in a language that seems strange from the contemporary perspective, his writings reflected assumptions about differences between the sexes that are not far removed from those widely held in the early twenty-first century and are expressed in a range of forums, including advice columns such as those above.

According to Ellis, women have a 'more complex sexual mechanism' than men that means that they are slower to arouse and that there are frequent difficulties in sexual relationships. As Ellis argued, while in 'man we have the more or less spontaneously erectile penis, which needs but very simple conditions to secure the ejaculation which brings relief... In women we have in the clitoris a corresponding apparatus on a small scale, behind [which] has developed a much more extensive mechanism, which also demands satisfaction, and requires for that satisfaction the presence of various conditions that are almost antagonistic' (1925: 235). Ellis explained this difference by reference to the analogy of the lock and key:

> We have to imagine a lock that not only requires a key to fit it, but should only be entered at the right moment, and, under the best conditions, may only become adjusted to the key by considerable use. The fact that the man takes the more active part in coitus has increased these difficulties; the woman is too often taught to believe that the whole function is low and impure, only to be submitted to at her husband's will and for his sake, and the man has no proper knowledge of the mechanism involved and the best way of dealing with it. The grossest brutality may thus be, and not infrequently is, exercised in all innocence by an ignorant husband who simply believes that he is performing his 'marital duties'. For a woman to exercise this physical brutality on a man is with difficulty possible; a man's pleasurable excitement is usually the necessary condition of the woman's sexual gratification. But the reverse if not the case, and, if the man is sufficiently ignorant or sufficiently coarse-grained to be satisfied with the woman's submission, he may easily become to her, in all innocence, a cause of torture. (Ellis, 1925: 235–236)

Ellis went on to explain that differences between men and women in sexual responses can result in women's indifference in relationships and 'frigidity'. Given that sexual excitement in women 'much more frequently requires to be actively aroused', Ellis believed that courtship is crucial in bringing about the 'necessary condition for sexual intercourse' (1925: 239–240). Courtship is functional, and has a dramatic quality, and is oriented to 'bring[ing] about in the most effectual manner the ultimate union of the sexes' (1925: 229). Ellis also suggested that the sexual impulse becomes stronger after sexual relationships are established. Making reference to observations of animals, he argued that women developed their 'maximum climax of sexual emotion' at a later age than men. Evidence of this was to be found in the fact that the 'most passionate love letters' of women were written by those 'who have passed, sometimes long passed, their first youth' (1925: 242). While men's sexual pleasure is 'intensive', in women it is 'extensive', which can be explained by the fact that the role of the male in procreation 'is confined to the ejaculation of semen into the vagina', while women are the child-bearers. Finally, in women, the sexual impulse shows a 'more marked tendency to periodicity than in men', over the short term (which is explained by menstruation), and over the longer term (reflecting changes in the reproductive life cycle).

This account of sexual difference, which posits men as the active partner and women as passive in sex, of different sexual cycles, and of sexual difficulties arising from the insensitivity of the male partner has been a common theme in writings of love, intimacy and sex since the late nineteenth century. The use of the lock-and-key analogy expresses powerfully the view that the roles of the male and females sexes are naturally complementary and reflects the 'phallo-centric' assumption that sexual fulfilment can only be derived from penetrative sex. The reference to the role of the courtship ritual in bringing about a successful sexual union is also significant in light of the aforementioned discourse of romantic love, with its focus on mutual attraction of the sexes. What separated humans, or at least Europeans, from animals in matters of sex were the codes of romantic love, including courtship, declarations of love, and marriage. Tellingly, after examining studies of 'the sexual instinct in savages', Ellis con-cluded that the sexual instinct had increased with the growth of civilisation and had become 'intimately connected with moral feelings' (Ellis, 1925: 276). The impulse of sex, which involved the idealisa-tion of each sex to the other, 'draws men and women together and holds them together' (1925: 276). Ellis believed that the conditions of civilisation – including a regular supply of good food, along with 'other stimulating factors available and exercised in modern commu-nities' – increased reproductive capacity and the ability of women to conceive 'almost at any time during the reproductive period'. That is, the conditions of reproduction are seen to provide the foundation for 'civilised' socio-sexual arrangements and the formation of com-plementary or 'opposite' sex roles.

Complementarity and the public/private distinction

As Shields argues, the idea of the complementarity of the sexes has been the ideal way to explain how variation could co-exist with the continuity and stability of the species (2002: 71). Sex differences in chemical processes that underpin, for example, differences in emotional make-up, are seen as 'functional' for the human species. Certain kinds of emotion are seen as more typical of one sex and purported sex-related differences are automatically ascribed as natural and functional. As Shields argues, the development of the model of complementary sex differences in intellectual and psychological attributes was bound up with the general movement in the nineteenth century towards belief in functional complementarity reflected in the private sphere/public sphere dichtomisation of woman/ man, family/work, and consumption/production (2002: 71–72). Since the time of Havelock Ellis, and especially since the late 1960s and 'second-wave' feminist politics, the significance of the private/public dichotomy for the definition and reinforcement of sex differences and inequalities has become increasingly apparent. As many writers have indicated, the public sphere, which is the world of work and public service, is associated with the masculine, whereas the private sphere, the world of domestic and intimate relations, is coded feminine. The public/private dichotomy is seen to correspond closely with a gender division of labour: men dominate the world of productive paid work, bureaucracy, and rational action, while women, who are primarily located in the private sphere, assume control over unpaid work in the family, intimate relations, and affective issues (see Chapter 1). However, the question of where to draw the boundary between the 'public' and the 'private' is by no means uncontentious; indeed, the construction of the boundary is a political act in itself (Yul-Davis, 1997: 80). Nevertheless, in academic and more general discussions about gender differences in conceptions of love, intimacy and sex as in discussions about other gender issues, there is widespread explicit or implicit agreement that this dichotomy is significant in defining and structuring gender relations. Thus, since these issues are seen as essentially 'private' matters, as matters of 'choice' between individuals that are played out largely in private spaces, they tend to be seen as essentially 'women's work' since, as noted, love is a feminised concept. However, the self-evidence of this dichotomy has been brought into question as a consequence of the growing proportion of dual-earner couples and feminist politics. Increasingly, 'private' (i.e. hidden) issues such as male-to-female sexual coercion, rape in marriage, child abuse, domestic violence and informal care, have been highlighted as 'public' issues for debate and action. A sphere that has been culturally defined as a matter of the autonomous action of individuals and as free from the interventions of the state has come to be viewed as a topic of public concern and subject to control through policy.

In recent years, the dynamics of sexual relationships has been the focus of particular attention among feminist researchers. Feminists have explored how the *gender system* has enabled men and women to perform certain prescribed 'feminine' or 'masculine' intimate and sexual behaviours. As Lewis argues, viewing gender as a socio-cultural system that implicates men and women in its reproduction is more useful for engaging men and women in rethinking the terms of masculinity and femininity than theoretical models that position women as victims of oppressive men who are in need of special attention and support (2002: 24). Questioning the meanings of intimacy has been central to feminist critical work. In recent sociological work, such as that undertaken by Giddens (1992), 'intimacy' has been viewed as a relatively unproblematic and gender-neutral category of experience and mode of expression. However, as Jamieson argues, at any given time, the ways and degrees of being intimate can vary enormously both *within* and *between* societies (Jamieson, 1998: 7). The idea of 'disclosing intimacy', and its promotion as an important part of an individual's well-being and of good relationships, has come into being only relatively recently. Love can take many forms, and 'disclosing intimacy' is not the only type of intimacy to be found in primary or personal relationships. There are many possible stories about intimacy and its connections with love and sex (Jamieson, 1998: 8–9, 106–135). As Jamieson observes, many of these stories are gender-specific. The adage that men seek sex and women seek intimacy – reiterated in the excerpt above – is one such story (Jamieson, 1998: 9). These stories find expression in the conduct of personal relationships, and in men's and women's different self-presentations and disclosures. As Jagger (2001) notes, although contemporary consumer culture provides individuals with important cultural resources for creating personal identities, these resources are not equally available to men and women. In her study of dating advertisements in the mid-1990s, Jagger found that gender stereotypes of appropriate femininity and masculinity persisted, and that women have a more restrictive repertoire of scripts available to them than men. Thus, in their self-advertisements, women tend to emphasise the characteristics traditionally associated with normative femininity such as their physical attractiveness, their caring and nurturing capacities, their 'warmth' and ability to listen (Jagger, 2001: 47–51). In the work of Giddens and other sociologists there is little recognition of how the gender system shapes how men and women 'perform intimacy'; how they present themselves to the other, and what, and how, they disclose to each other.

'Sex work'

Feminist researchers have also drawn attention to women's sexual subordination and 'sex work' undertaken in heterosexual 'intimate' relationships. To call sex within intimate relationships 'work' would seem to greatly disturb a deeply held notion that sex is 'naturally' pleasurable and expressive of love. However, feminist sociologists have highlighted how men and women differently experience sex in relationships and how, in particular, women manage feelings of distaste and disappointment in long-term heterosexual relationships – the transition between what are conventionally assumed to be the two phases of 'love', 'falling in love' to a stable 'companionate love' – by, for example, negotiating the degree of intimacy. Duncombe and Marsden (2002), in their study of 'sex work' in long-term heterosexual relationships, for example, showed how women and men dealt with the difficulties posed by the gap between what they believed sex 'ought' to be and the reality of dealing with their different sexual desires and expectations over the longer term. They discovered, among things, that men and women had different views on the use of pornography in their relationship, for livening up sex that had 'lost its passion', and of the significance of masturbation (2002: 235–236). Duncombe and Marsden (1993) found that many women express unhappiness in what they perceived to be men's unwillingness or incapacity to be involved in emotional intimacy which they saw as necessary to sustain close couple relationships. The women whom they interviewed felt that they took the major responsibility for their emotional lives, including persuading their husbands (who often buried themselves in their work) to father their children. As a response, the women had built an emotional life apart from their husbands, through children, part-time work and relationships with other women (Duncombe and Marsden, 1993: 225–226). Such research reveals not only the asymmetry between the sexes in emotional work that is obscured by the ideal of romantic love but also suggests the different 'investments' of men and women in their 'intimate' relationships. That is, in undertaking a disproportionate share of such emotional work, women reveal that they tend to have more at stake in a lasting relationship.

That the gender system in the West at least allows much greater scope for the separation of sex and love for men than for women has been highlighted by feminist research on the practices of prostitution, sex tourism (otherwise known as prostitution tourism), and pornography. Most of these practices involve a 'purely' economic relationship; that is, payment by men for the use of the bodies, or the consumption of the images of the bodies, of women or children, with whom they do *not* have close, loving relations. Prostitution, of course, has a long history in many societies, which is taken by some feminists to indicate the universality of the sexual exploitation of women; the reduction of women to passive desiring/desirable bodies. However, feminists such as Mary McIntosh have challenged the assumption that men's sexual desire is natural and inevitable, which reinforces the idea that women are passive recipients of male sexual needs (Evans, 1997: 93–94). Consequently, much feminist attention has focused on the economic and social systems underpinning prostitution. Linda Grant offers a commonly voiced feminist perspective on the political economy of prostitution. In asking why, despite changes in gender politics since the 1960s, 'there is no evidence that any sex industry aimed at women exists', she argues that 'the male experience of prostitution since the sexual revolution is increasingly bound up with control. Money, paying for things, confers power, and men have lost some power in women's recent acquisition of it' (1991: 31). Sex tourism is another practice of sexual exploitation, by men, from predominantly rich, developed countries, of women, from mainly poor, developing countries. Since the 1960s, many packaged tours have been marketed exclusively to men, particularly to Southeast Asian countries, which have been promoted as 'a male paradise' (Muroi and Sasaki, 1997: 180). As a practice that also involves a financial exchange, albeit with the assistance of third-party intermediaries, sex tourism is seen to 'objectify' women by separating love from desire and sex. It can be considered part of a system of sexual slavery that has operated on an international level for centuries (see, e.g. Barry, 1979). The sexual relationship between prostitute and client has been described as mirroring the relationship between the developing and developed world, with women in the poorest regions often attracted from their local area to the urban service sector, including the tourism industry by the promise of higher earnings (Muroi and Sasaki, 1997: 193–194; see also various contributions in Manderson and Jolly, 1997).

Feminists have been more divided in their views on pornography. While some feminists have wanted to legally regulate pornography on the grounds that it denigrates women or have lobbied for legislation that would enable women to bring action against pornographers or pornography on the basis that they/it harmed them (see Wilson, 1992: 18), other scholars have warned of the dangers of equating all pornography with sexism, especially given the changing definitions of 'pornography' and different perspectives on the nature of sexuality. A number of the contributors to Segal and McIntosh's, *Sex Exposed: Sexuality and the Pornography Debate* (1992), published in a wake of HIV/AIDS, argue for the need to acknowledge the social construction of sexuality and the desires and discontents of both men and women, and the dangers of censoring sexually explicit material (e.g. Gorna, 1992; McIntosh, 1992; Segal, 1992). (The AIDS theorist and campaigner, Simon Watney, among others, has cautioned against the censoring of pornography on the grounds that 'it' is *intrinsically* obscene, arguing that this plays into the right-wing moral agenda and involves an intensification of the moral management by various authorities of 'dangerous sexualities' [1997: 59–61].) In the late twentieth and early twenty-first centuries, the Internet and cable TV have helped make pornography ubiquitous (Marriott and Mondino, 2003), raising novel questions for feminists. While some writers claim that this has allowed women to take greater control of the sex industry, as video producers – for example, the theme of the film, *Sex Empires*, shown on UK's BBC2 in November 2003 – it can be argued that this is merely an assertion of women's economic independence rather than an effort to develop a feminist sex industry. New media may have created new opportunities for the production and consumption of sexual imagery; however, romantic ideals continue to provide a significant reference point for men and women in living their lives and conducting their relationships.

Conclusion

The discourses of romantic love have had a profound impact on conceptions of the person and of gender. Our strong feelings for particular others seem natural and unique to us and yet are described and expressed in ways which mirror the ideals, values, and distinctions of the society in which we live. The notion of passionate love as an irrational, overpowering force arose at a particular point in history and takes its meaning in opposition to an assumed dispassionate rationality, or lack of concern or care for the other. This distinction between passionate and dispassionate finds its counterpart in the duality of femininity and masculinity. That is, women's and men's roles in love are seen as different, but complementary. 'Opposite sexes' are seen to naturally attract, the assumption being that same sex attraction is 'unnatural'. The romantic notion of love, in other words, has an implicit heterosexual bias. These ideals, values, and oppositions have governed relations between men and women, and shaped their capacities to empathise with, and to give pleasure to, or receive pleasure from, the other. Thus, the norms of masculinity enable men to separate sex from love ('take sex'), while the norms of femininity prescribe that women 'give love'. Despite recent changes in the norms governing intimate relationships, as a consequence of an increasingly pervasive consumerism and market rationality in everyday life, as argued, the romantic ideal continues to shape thinking about sex/gender differences. The recurring theme of this book, that emotions are 'engendered', however, suggests that there is nothing inevitable about gender constructions. In the next and final chapter, I explore prospects for change in conceptions of gender in the light of the growing attention to emotion and 'emotional literacy' in a number of contemporary societies.

5
Gender, 'Emotional Literacy', and the Future

By nature, a man is suspicious, competitive, controlled, defensive and a loner who hides his emotional state to stay in control. For men, becoming emotional is seen as being out of control...As a nest-defender, a woman's brain is pre-wired to be open, trusting, co-operative, show vulnerability, reveal emotions and know it's not necessary to stay in control all the time. This is why a man and woman encounter problems together, each is confused about the other's reaction.

— Pease and Pease (2001)

We all value social relationships, but are there differences in what each sex values about other people? Women tend to value the development of altruistic, reciprocal relationships. Such relationships require good empathizing skills. In contrast, men tend to value power, politics and competition. This pattern is found across widely different cultures and historical periods, and is even found among chimpanzees.

— Baron-Cohen (2003)

Despite persuasive feminist arguments and considerable evidence to the contrary, the idea that men and women have different emotional make-ups and dispositions, and that this difference is 'natural' and universal, endures in many contemporary societies. This assumption informs many policies and practices in the 'public' sphere, including in schools and workplaces, and shapes people's views and conduct in the most 'private', 'intimate' aspects of their lives. This book has reviewed just some prevailing gender–emotion associations and how they may shape the experiences of individual men and women. Whether in the institutions of the military, the theatres of war, the spheres of love, intimacy and sex, or the workplace, men and women are seen to be constituted in ways that make certain patterns of conduct and problems seem inevitable. However, it has become increasingly apparent that these associations are neither permanent nor universal. The significance of emotion for definitions of masculinity and femininity and for how men and women perceive and conduct themselves may vary considerably through time and across contexts. To use dramaturgical language, both the gender scripts, and how men and women enact those scripts, are diverse. Men and women may express and conduct themselves in ways which, from a contemporary Western standpoint, are deemed to be non gender-typical. Further, the category of emotion itself is 'engendered': how we think about and evaluate 'emotion', what we believe constitutes an 'emotional' experience, and how we as individuals respond 'emotionally', is shaped by prevailing views on gender, which in turn are influenced by history and socio-cultural and political contexts. It is clear that 'emotion' is imbued with strong evaluative connotations. Emotionality tends to be associated with femininity, while rationality is linked with masculinity, with the former generally accorded less value than the latter in modern Western societies at least. Work involving considerable emotional content (particularly caring) is in the main defined as 'women's work', while work involving a high degree of rational input and 'emotional detachment' is generally seen to be 'men's work'. These associations and evaluations inform public discourse about gender and difference and profoundly shape people's life chances and subjectivity or 'sense of self'.

This chapter focuses on the implications for conceptions of gender and gender difference of a recent focus on emotion and 'emotional literacy' in a number of contemporary societies. According to its proponents, 'emotional literacy' promises a range of benefits for the individual and society, including reduced school dropouts and better educational outcomes, less aggressive and destructive behaviour, enhanced empathy, and improved relationships. Men and boys are seen to especially benefit from improved 'emotion management', and have consequently been the target of a number of recent policies and programmes. It is argued that many problems, including violent behaviours and relationship difficulties, arise from the inability of men and boys to adequately deal with and properly express their emotions. 'Emotional literacy' programmes are seen to have the potential to make men and boys more caring, less aggressive, and better able to relate to others. What can we make of this focus on 'emotional literacy', particularly as it relates to men and boys, in the light of recent economic, social, and political changes underway in a number of contemporary societies? Does 'emotional literacy' have the potential to deliver the benefits that are promised and perhaps reduce purported emotional differences between men and women? This chapter critically examines the politics of 'emotional literacy', particularly as it pertains to ideas of gender and gender difference. It points to some limitations of recent debates about 'difference' and the contributions of 'nature' and 'nurture' to the production of difference. The chapter concludes by suggesting some foci for future critical work and arguing the need for a more explicitly 'emotion-focused' gender studies. Before proceeding further, however, it is worth reminding the reader of the assumptions that have guided this analysis from the outset.

This book begins from the premise that 'emotion' plays a crucial role in the governance of social life in modern Western societies. In Chapter 1, I referred to the work of Reddy (2001) who contends that, for a political regime to endure, it must establish a normative order for the expression of emotions – what he calls an 'emotional regime'. In his view, how emotions are regulated reveals much about a society's views of human nature and human possibilities. As Reddy argues, emotional regimes vary according to the amount of liberty accorded to the individual, the required forms of self-control, the strategies of emotional management, and the penalties for violating norms. Different times and different contexts provide different opportunities for emotional experience and expression. There is likely to be a large variety of emotional styles in contemporary societies, with class, gender, and ethnic variation being exploited to sustain the division of labour. I have suggested that, although Reddy has little to say about gender or gender relations, his work is a useful starting point in analysing gender–emotion associations, since it draws attention to the ways in which broader political regimes may shape and limit gender-based emotional expression and self-definition or 'identity'. If one acknowledges that emotion – its definition, its experience and its expression – is a manifestation of power relations and has political implications then an important task for critical scholars is to reveal how 'emotion' has been mobilised to fulfil certain governmental objectives and what this reveals about conceptions of self and society and prospects for change in relation to gender.

The politics of 'emotional literacy'

In recent years, the emotions and how they are expressed have been the focus of a growing number of policies and programmes in a number of countries. From the 1990s, an emerging body of literature, with contributions from various academic fields, has emphasised the importance of the emotions, for health, for intimate relationships, for education, for work, for the economy, and for the nation. More and more, our emotional lives – long *portrayed* as private and hence beyond power and politics, but in reality always subject to regulation – have become an *explicit* focus of debate and public action. A whole new array of expertise has been applied to the task of understanding and addressing 'emotional deficits', encompassing more and more areas of life, including workplaces, schools, and homes. Citizens are called upon to 'get in touch' with their emotions, and to become 'emotionally literate', for the sake of their own health and well-being and for the advancement of economic prosperity and social cohesion. Promoting the ideal of 'emotional intelligence', and 'opening our feelings' to others, has become an obligation of citizenship, a means by which one can demonstrate one's membership of, and active contribution to, 'society'. Daniel Goleman's *Emotional Intelligence* (1995) has been an especially influential reference point in discussions about emotion and its role in personal and social distress. His writings on the problem of 'emotional illiteracy' and how this may be addressed provide some insight into a number of the underlying concerns and assumptions in this discourse on emotions. The commercial success of this book, and its influence in shaping policies and practices, suggest that the ideas therein resonate strongly with broader concerns about the current state of emotional life.

In his book, Goleman blames a range of problems, including growing rates of depression and 'a surging tide of aggression', on a widespread 'emotional ineptitude, desperation, and recklessness' in 'our families, our communities, and our collective lives' (1995: x). Drawing on recent scientific studies of emotion, Goleman argues for the importance of nurturing 'emotional intelligence', which he describes as 'abilities' which include 'self-control, zeal and persistence, and the ability to motivate oneself' (1995: xii). As he notes, 'these skills...can be taught to children, giving them a better chance to use whatever intellectual potential the genetic lottery may have given them' (1995: xii). By properly managing our emotions, readers are informed, we will be better equipped to handle the challenges that we face in life. The problem, as Goleman sees it, is not so much an absence of emotions, but rather the failure of people to adequately regulate, control, and channel emotions, to make them more effective, less stressed and healthier, as well as better communicators. Without such control, emotion will rule our lives, override our rationality, and impede our effectiveness. As Goleman explains, 'Whether it be in controlling impulse and putting off gratification, regulating our moods so they facilitate rather than impede thinking, motivating ourselves to persist and try, try again in the face of setbacks, or finding ways to enter flow and so perform more effectively – all bespeak the power of emotion to guide effective effort' (1995: 95). Emotions that are out of control, Goleman argues, can become 'toxic', leading to stress, depression, suicide, and other complaints (1995: 168–176). Readers are called upon to develop greater self-awareness of their moods and thoughts about their moods, so as they are better able to act to change their feelings. They should cease being 'slaves' to their distressing emotions (e.g. 'chronic worries', 'depression') for the sake of their 'emotional well-being, and develop a 'master aptitude', that is, channel their emotions towards a productive end (1995: 46–95). Although we cannot change our genetic heritage, 'which endows each of us with a series of emotional set-points that determines our temperament', we can do much to shape the 'emotional habits that govern our lives' (1995: xiii).

In Goleman's view, our rational actions are subject to 'neural hijackings' or 'emotional explosions', which originate in the amygdala, 'a centre of the limbic brain'. The amygdala, Goleman explains, is a 'repository for emotional memory' which can trigger a 'fight-or-flight' type emotional response that can sometimes have detrimental implications. While feelings are 'indispensable for rational decisions', they can also disrupt 'the most "rational" decision-making' and become 'toxic'. For example, stress ('anxiety out of proportion and out of place'), if uncontrolled, can lead to sickness and affect the course of recovery (Goleman, 1995: 21–29, 168–185). The task, then, is to 'reeducate the emotional brain' through various means (e.g. relaxation techniques, 'retelling and reconstructing the story of the trauma') and increase 'emotional literacy' by, for example, making the emotions topics of study in school (1995: Chapters 13, 16). Goleman's work reflects a long-held view on the emotions, which suggest that they may exert a *power over* us and have the potential to disrupt and rule our lives – evident, for example, in the case of sexual or romantic love (see Chapter 4). That is, if we do not learn to manage our emotions, then they will manage us.

The call for emotional self-mastery reflects a 'masculinist' bias in Western culture: emotionality, which is associated with the body and coded feminine, is seen to potentially threaten rationality, which is associated with the mind and coded masculine. As noted in Chapter 1, the rhetoric of control has been a theme in discussions about emotions and reflects the view of emotions as natural, irrational, and dangerous. The basic 'fight-or-flight type emotional response', described by Goleman, represents the embodied threat to our rational, controlled selves, which is in need of control. Goleman's call for improved 'emotional management' and 'schooling the emotions' reveals a conception of self as disembodied, reflective, active, and entrepreneurial. It implies the need for detailed work on the self, in order that one may become more disciplined, resilient and better able to effectively utilise that which is taken to be pre-given; that is, our biological make-up. This particular conception of self closely approximates that which has been promoted through a range of policies during a period of rapid and radical economic and social welfare reform, namely, advanced liberalism, and is manifest in many spheres of contemporary social life (see Chapters 1, 4). That is, we are required to 'change with the times', become 'more flexible', and 'adapt', and link our personal goals with social goals. Those who fail to link their personal fulfilment to social reform are categorised as 'problems', as lacking 'self-esteem', or charged with 'anti-social behaviour', and are called upon to undertake training, education, or therapy (see, e.g. Cruikshank, 1996). Since the publication of Goleman's book, the teaching of 'emotional intelligence' or 'emotional literacy' has been promoted by many educators, corporate leaders, psychotherapists, and activist groups.

In recent years, Emotional Intelligence has developed into an established field of study in its own right, which is seen to have applications in health, business, the workplace, and intimate relationships (see, e.g. Ciarrochi, *et al.*, 2001). In 2003, the UK's Department for Education and Skills (DfES) endorsed the teaching of emotional skills, with a strategy to be piloted across 250 schools across the country. For some years, a number of schools have incorporated emotional literacy into their curricula, including anger management groups, anti-bullying training and seminars in emotional intelligence 'for everyone from the governor to the playground attendant' (Raafat, 2003). A study undertaken in 2002 by Southampton University, on behalf of DfES, found that 'the experts' whom they interviewed from the 'key organisations and agencies working in the field of emotional and social competence and wellbeing' expressed a strong belief in the value of promoting emotional and social competence and wellbeing at national, local education authority (LEA), and school levels. The report of the study also documented a range of benefits from the literature, including 'greater educational and work success, improved behaviour, increased inclusion, improved learning, greater social cohesion, increased social capital, and improvements to mental health' (Weare and Gray, 2003: 6). The researchers noted that, 'The acceptance of emotion, the building of warm relationships and the need for active and empathic communication were seen by all those interviewed as being at the heart of the processes of fostering emotional and social competence and wellbeing' (Weare and Gray, 2003: 57).

Some of the ways in which LEA managers and experts saw organisations as fostering warm relationships included:

- putting relationships at the heart of the organisation
- feeling comfortable with the expression of emotion and taking the emotional component into account when considering all processes and decision-making
- good communication, especially active listening
- the development of key qualities such as empathy, respect, genuineness and authenticity and trust
- people being and feeling valued as individuals and having a sense of belonging. (Weare and Gray, 2003: 57)

The DfES has offered assistance to teachers and 'practitioners in early years settings' in developing 'social, emotional, and behavioural skills', by producing 'resources' such as guidance booklets, reference materials (e.g. posters, photographs, and photocopiable resources) and 'a set of cards giving ideas for whole-school assemblies and class-based activities' (DfES, 2003: 5). A guidance package designed for teachers notes that children who have developed such skills, and 'are educated within an environment supportive to emotional health and well-being', will be motivated and have skills to: 'be effective and successful learners, make and sustain relationships; deal with and resolve conflict effectively and fairly; solve problems with others or by themselves; manage strong feelings such as frustration, anger and anxiety; recover from setbacks and persist in the face of difficulties; work and play cooperatively; compete fairly and win and lose with dignity and respect for competitors; recognise and stand up for their rights and the rights of others; [and] understand and value the difference between people, respecting the right of others to have beliefs and values different from their own' (DfES, 2003: 5–6).

The belief that there are broad social benefits to be derived from the schooling of the emotions has also been endorsed by Antidote: Campaign for Emotional Literacy and The National Emotion Interest Group. A website, http:www.antidote.org.uk/html/about.htm explains that Antidote 'was set up in 1997 to work for the vision of an emotionally literate society where the facility to handle the complexities of emotional life is as widespread as the capacity to read, write and do arithmetic'. It notes:

> Antidote recognises that change is a constant of modern life. Managed well it stimulates energy and excitement. Too often, though, it leads to stress, disaffection and poor relationships. Antidote believes that emotional literacy can ensure people have a positive experience of change. Emotional literacy is the practice of thinking individually and collectively about how emotions shape our actions, and of using emotional understanding to enrich our thinking.

Here again one can see evidence of belief in the potentially disruptive power of the emotions and in the ability to harness them for benefit, in this case for the 'positive experience' of change. Emotional management is seen as something that can advantage everyone, at a time when the constancy of change has the potential to disrupt personal lives and relationships. The objectives of this 'Campaign' have a democratic flavour about them. As its website notes, Antidote seeks to achieve its goals by: (1) Developing good practice in the enhancement of emotional literacy; (2) Demonstrating the benefits of emotional literacy through action research; and (3) Disseminating these findings widely through 'emotional literacy audits', conferences, training, consultancy, and publications. It notes that its 'mission statement is to promote emotional literacy across *all sections of society*' (http: www.antidote.org.uk/html/about.htm; emphases added). To promote its aims, it has published *The Emotional Literacy Handbook*, based on 'a six-year investigation into how schools can use emotional literacy to improve achievement, behaviour and well-being'. The book outlines the purported successes of schooling in emotional literacy, including increased student motivation and participation in learning, reduced behavioural problems, improved communication between students and teachers, and an increased capacity among students 'to deal with the emotions that can render them unable to learn, and to access emotional states that lead to a richer experience of learning'.

The National Emotion Interest Group has a similarly ambitious, democratising, goal. On its website, Nelig.com, the Group claims that it, 'is dedicated to *the promotion of emotional literacy for everyone . . . adults and children alike*'. (emphases added) It notes that, 'Our aim is to promote and resource emotional literacy defined as, "the ability to recognise, understand, handle and appropriately express emotions".' The site includes a range of resources, including articles on emotional literacy, assessment tools, web links to local emotional literacy groups, and information on emotional literacy conferences and courses. It also includes a 'friends of nelig', which includes educational psychologists, senior/specialist educational psychologists, principal educational psychologists, companies/organisations, self-employed (consultants, psychologists, etc.), parents, head/deputy headteachers, advisory teachers, non-teaching school staff (school counsellors, site managers, etc.), and 'other' interested parties. This extensive list of interested parties reveals the extent of contemporary concern with the promotion of 'emotional literacy' as a personal and social benefit. The entries make reference to a wide variety of activities and strategies to advance 'emotional literacy', including training programmes, workshops, lectures, and research projects. Many of these activities are oriented to educators working with children and young people in schools and other settings, but some are oriented to managers working in the public and private sectors. Visitors to the website are invited to contribute to the goals of Nelig., by submitting news items or articles on emotional literacy, details of any emotional literacy events in which they are involved, 'project notes' ('Short, informal reflections on pieces of work you have been involved in or just brief, factual accounts of initiatives in your area'), information on courses on emotional literacy or emotional intelligence they wish to be advertised, and details of local emotional literacy interest groups they may be involved with and that they wish to be advertised. If they wish, they can become 'a friend' of Nelig. In short, all are invited to contribute to the project of enhancing 'emotional literacy', which is presented as a self-evidently valuable goal for self and society. The portrayal of 'emotional literacy' as a democratic endeavour is assisted by the use of an inclusive language and the provision of a 'user-friendly' website and forums designed to allow wide participation.

The emotional lives of men and boys

Although those who promote 'emotional literacy' see benefits for all, the emotional lives of men and boys have been a particular focus of many policy initiatives and research projects. In recent years, men's emotions have been the subject of a burgeoning scholarly literature, with contributions from disciplines such as psychology, sociology, anthropology, and feminist studies. For many feminist and masculinity scholars, men's 'disconnection from their emotions' results in a plethora of problems: loss of spontaneity, difficulties in loving and nurturing others, 'emotional dumping' on partners and family members, 'inappropriate' emotional reactions to certain situations, including aggressive and violent behaviour towards others, self-harm, accidents, and mental and physical illness (e.g. Harris, 1995; Helgeson, 1995; Seidler, 1989, 1997). The need to address men's emotional lives has consequently been highlighted in both recent gender politics and government policies. Theoretical perspectives are diverse, sometimes locating men's emotional lives within a broader sociological framework (e.g. the Enlightenment coupling of masculinity with reason, or global politico-economic forces) (Connell, 1995, 2000; Seidler, 1997) but very often make extensive reference to the theories and concepts of psychology, psychoanalysis, and neuroscience (e.g. Chodorow, 1999; Fischer, 2000). Much of this work therefore resonates strongly with a more general psychological and biological reductionism and therapeutic and 'self-help' emphasis in many contemporary societies. It is suggested or implied that if men can 'reconnect' or 'get in touch' with, or 'discipline' their emotions this will not only allow them to live healthier and fuller lives but will also benefit their partners, families, and the broader society. In some writings, men are portrayed as inhabiting a separate emotional reality from women which results in communication difficulties and conflicts in relationships – perhaps most evident in John Gray's highly popular book, *Men are from Mars, Women are from Venus* (1992). Men are presented as less empathetic and less able to control their emotions. Goleman, himself, has offered some suggestions as to these apparent sex differences. In Goleman's view, men are the more emotionally 'vulnerable sex' – partly because they are more prone to 'neural hijackings', which leads to 'stonewalling' as a defensive response, but also because women, in pursuing their roles as emotional managers, are 'more likely to criticise their husbands'. The differences in how men and women deal with feelings often leads to an escalation of tension in emotional relationships and consequently relationship breakdowns. However, Goleman believes that difficulties can be overcome by adopting a number of strategies, such as self-monitoring and 'reframing' one's thoughts ('detoxifying self-talk') and adopting 'nondefensive listening and speaking' (e.g. 'hearing the feelings behind what is being said') (see Goleman, 1995: 130–147).

Boys' emotions are the focus of many special education programmes. More and more it has been recognised that boys have difficulty expressing their emotions or express them 'inappropriately' and that this may detrimentally affect their learning, leading to a decline in their performance relative to girls, and stifling emotional development in later years. The task, as many educators see it, is to educate boys to 'recognise', 'get in touch' with, and control their emotions. Kindlon and Thompson's *Raising Cain: Protecting the Emotional Life of Boys* (1999) is indicative of this concern to address the 'deficit' in boys' emotional lives. In their book, Kindlon and Thompson argue the case for teaching boys 'emotional literacy' – which they conceive as 'the ability to read and understand our emotions and those of others' (1999: 4). The authors, 'two male psychologists who have specialized in treating boys for more than thirty-five years of our combined practice', recount experiences of treating boys who are angry and aggressive, and 'boys who don't talk'. As they note, 'Some boys don't have the words for their feelings – *sad*, or *angry*, or *ashamed*, for instance' (1999: 4; original emphases). It is their view that 'our culture is railroading boys into lives of isolation, shame, and anger'. Their goal is to 'help them understand their emotional life and develop an emotional vocabulary' (1999: 4). In their view, while girls tend to get 'lots of encouragement from an early age to be emotionally literate', boys do not, which shows at a young age when they display their 'disregard for the feelings of others at home, at school, or in the playground' (1999: 5). Kindlon and Thompson ask,

> What do boys need to become emotionally literate? We think the answer is clear. Boys need an emotional vocabulary that expands their ability to express themselves in ways other than anger or aggression. They need to experience empathy at home and at school and be encouraged to use it if they are to develop conscience. Boys, no less than girls, need to feel emotional connections. Throughout their lives, but especially during adolescence, they need close, supportive relationships that can protect them from becoming victims of their turbulent, disowned emotions. Most important, a boy needs male modelling of a rich emotional life. He needs to learn emotional literacy as much from his father and other men as from his mother and other women, because he must create a life and language for himself that speak with male identity. He must see and believe that emotions belong in the life of a man. (Kindlon and Thompson, 1999: 7)

As with many other personal and social problems, the failure of boys' emotional management is often blamed on schools, and sometimes on a kind of reverse systemic discrimination against boys resulting from earlier feminist-inspired educational reforms that have benefited girls but have 'left boys behind'. According to the sociologist Bob Connell, boys' emotional and educational problems can in part be attributed to the 'gender regime' of schools, which includes its power relations, division of labour, patterns of emotion, and symbolism (2000: 153–154). While acknowledging that schools are not the only institutional influence on masculinities (in fact, he suggests that the childhood family, the adult workplace and sexual relationships are 'more potent' (2000: 146)), Connell believes that a school's 'gender regime' plays a significant role in shaping definitions of masculinities. These definitions, Connell contends, exist as 'social facts' which, although negotiable by pupils entering a school, nevertheless play a significant role in forging identity (2000: 154). Concerns about boys' 'failure' relative to girls, he notes, have led to a number of educational programmes on gender issues, and efforts to address dropout rates of boys; for example, African-American youth in the US (Connell, 2000: 148). However, while there been incessant calls from parents and teachers for urgent action, there remain a number of unanswered questions about how schools may influence the educational outcomes for boys and challenge constructions of masculinity. Connell believes that 'the processes of masculinity construction' work against the education of boys, or at least some groups of boys, by pushing them away from areas of knowledge which they ought to be in contact with, and by establishing a competitive environment which works against the nurturance of good human relationships (Connell, 2000: 160–169). He argues for new forms of pedagogy, including 'gender-specific' programmes, and institutional change (e.g. to accommodate timetable changes for such programmes in co-educational schools), as well as a greater involvement of parents, teachers, and communities in expanding education work on masculinity and programmes for boys (2000: 164–176).

These debates and claims about 'emotional deficits' and arguments for 'emotional literacy', although making references to and using the language of personal empowerment, participation, and social change, entail a number of assumptions that are questionable and, arguably, are politically conservative in their implications. For a start, the focus on 'emotional literacy' suggests the existence of a discrete realm of affective experience that is unaffected by social definitions and political influences. It denies how the normative order of a society may shape the expression of emotions (the 'emotional regime') and indeed what 'counts' as 'emotion'. At particular times and under certain conditions different types of affectivity may be either valued or devalued according to how they mesh with wider political goals. Both boys' and girls' emotional expression and conduct, both inside and outside the classroom, has been a focus of concern at different times, in response to a range of influences, including prevailing medical views on the treatment of problems and changes in government policies. Conrad and Schneider have shown, for example, how children's 'deviant' behaviour – defined as disruptive, disobedient, rebellious, antisocial, or 'emotionally disturbed' – became defined as a medical problem ('hyperkinesis' or 'hyperactivity') in the 1960s and 1970s, in the US, in response to the development of new medical mechanisms of social control and the influence of various agents outside medicine (e.g. groups promoting medical perspectives on child disability) (1992: 145–171). The assumption that relationship difficulties and problems have an 'emotional' basis locates supposed difficulties or problems inside the person rather than in socio-political contexts. Difficulties or 'problems' are blamed on individuals who are seen as needing 'correction'; that is, 'literacy'. The definition of problems as *literacy* problems legitimates a role for experts, or rather particular groups of experts, especially educators, psychologists, psychiatrists, and social workers, in the resolution of 'problems', and is consistent with a more general therapeutic orientation to the resolution of problems found in contemporary culture (see, e.g. Furedi, 2004). The drive to affect micro-reforms in curricula to advance 'emotional management' never leads to a consideration of how policies and programmes construct certain desirable identities or to a critical examination of the assumptions, ideologies, and practices underpinning educational systems. The question of why boys' emotions have recently become a specific concern to policy makers, educators, and others, and what this might reveal about power and politics and gender relations specifically, begs for examination.

The commodification of emotion: implications for gender

The growing emphasis on 'emotional literacy', particularly the 'emotional literacy' of boys, may be explained, at least in part, by reference to the particular significance attributed to emotional labour, or at least certain kinds of emotional labour, in late capitalist societies. As Hochschild (1983, 2003) has argued, in an advanced consumer society, characterised by a strong service sector, more and more people have their jobs defined in terms of meeting the needs of customers. Our relations in the workplace are restructured in terms of consumer–producer and purchaser–provider relations, which require the performance of certain kinds of affective work, that is, 'emotional labour', much of it face to face (see Chapter 1). Emotional labour has become a highly valued commodity, and a failure to express one's emotions in requisite ways is seen to impede the smooth functioning of capitalist enterprise. The ability to manage one's feelings through public observable facial and bodily displays is something that can be bought and sold for a wage and therefore has exchange value (Hochschild, 1983: 186). Emotional labour requires a range of skills, including those of good interpersonal communication, group working, and the ability to manage stress, to exhibit confidence, and to demonstrate an array of context-specific emotional competencies. For example, those in service occupations need to control anger and to show a smiling demeanour when dealing directly with customers. Schools and universities are required to play their part in producing citizens who can operate in customer-focused work environments and to demonstrate that they teach these skills. (Many, if not most, schools and universities are now subject to 'quality audits' that ensure that such skills are 'embedded' in courses.) As Hochschild notes, emotional labour involves acting a part, either through changing our outward appearance through the use of body language, that is, 'surface acting', or by 'deep acting', which involves altering one's feelings so that one expresses feeling spontaneously (1983: 35–39). Such acting can involve costs. While 'surface acting' is unproblematic for those obliged to be engaged in it in that it is a superficial performance, and is recognised as such (e.g. service workers wishing us a nice day, to which we reciprocate politely), 'deep acting' can damage the individual and interpersonal relations. For example, 'over-identification' with a job may lead one to suffer stress and be susceptible to burnout, and/or to become remote and detached from those they serve (1983: 186–189).

Different jobs require different kinds and degrees of 'emotional labour', and consequently impose different demands on the self in terms of 'surface acting' or 'deep acting'. Further, work contexts vary in terms of the provision of emotional training needs. As Aldridge (2003) notes, while some workplaces may offer formal training in emotional labour (e.g. airline companies), in others (e.g. caring professions) emotional labour is learnt on the job or seen to come 'naturally' to employees, especially if they are women. Given the gendered division of labour in the service sector, with women occupying the greater proportion of front-line jobs in paid service work, they face particular demands in emotional labour and arguably are at most risk of suffering its ill effects. In Britain, in 2003, women occupied the vast majority of roles in administrative and secretarial occupations

(79 per cent), personal service occupations (83 per cent), and sales and customer service (68 per cent). The women working in these occupational groups comprise 48 per cent of the total female workforce (Women and Equality Unit, 2004). Despite the often high emotional labour demanded by these jobs, many are part time and poorly paid. A pay gap between men and women can be attributed to women's much greater role in caring and other service work and to taking career breaks to look after their families (Walby and Olsen, 2002). (Women are more likely than men to be in part time employment in any field because they shoulder the greater responsibility for unpaid care. Of those in employment, 42 per cent of women work part time compared with 9 per cent of men [Women and Equality Unit, 2004].) The traditionally 'female' jobs are those which often lack autonomy and are insecure, and are frequently under the direct surveillance and control of others, especially men. They are often 'open floor' jobs that by their nature involve only a limited transfer of knowledge from men to women (Spain, 1992: 206). In many instances, women are obliged to perform a kind of 'hand-maiden' role to their male supervisors or bosses.

Of course, these employment statistics tell us nothing about the substantial *unpaid* or poorly paid service work, particularly caring work, performed largely by women in and outside the home. Policies of de-institutionalisation in recent decades, with a new emphasis on the private home as the most appropriate context for care, has meant that women have shouldered an increasing burden of such work (Cant, 1994). A considerable amount of the work undertaken outside the institutions of paid work, however, is undertaken in non-home settings such as nursing homes, charities, churches, and voluntary organisations, where the contribution, though perhaps locally recognised, is largely undocumented and unacknowledged in public discourses about work and often not addressed or inadequately addressed in government policies. While women who undertake unpaid work at home or in these settings may enjoy more autonomy and more control over their work than those in paid work settings, they are likely to face another set of demands. Caring work, specifically, requires a range of personal qualities such as 'empathy, patience and a capacity for detailed attention to the needs of others' (Watson and Mears, 1999: 3). Watson and Mears found in their study of the experience of caring for the elderly that, for the majority of care workers, caring transforms the life of the carer and shapes 'all activities, relation-ships, plans, ambitions, and choices'. As they note, 'It was a constant preoccupation; there was no shrugging off the concern or putting the worry to one side' (1999: 63). As more and more women in Western countries undertake paid labour outside the home, and face strong pressures to conform to the male pattern of work (competing with fellow professionals, building a reputation, minimising family work by finding someone else to do it, and so on), a growing proportion of the burden of this 'emotional labour' of care is shouldered by women from poor countries who are searching for better opportunities and higher pay in the developed world (Ehrenreich and Hochschild, 2002). Thus, the male pattern of work is contributing to a global division of 'emotional labour', involving the redistribution of 'emotional resources' from poor countries to rich ones (2002: 15–30).

The gendered division of labour presents a different set of emotional demands for men. These demands are associated with the organ-isational cultures which are generally dominated by men. Statistics reveal that men are more likely to occupy managerial and senior official positions than women, which are often 'close door' and tend to favour a certain style of emotional expression. In 2003, of all men of working age in employment, 18 per cent were in such positions, whereas the equivalent for women was 10 per cent. They are also much more represented in skilled trades occupations (20 per cent of all men of working age in employment, compared with 2 per cent of women), and to work as process, plant and machine operatives (12 per cent as opposed to 3 per cent) (Women and Equality Unit, 2004) which, again, entail particular emotional demands. Many managers and senior officials will be required to work on a face-to-face basis with customers/clients and to effectively manage interpersonal relation-ships with and between employees, whereas fewer labourers and machine operators will be expected to. However, the kind and extent of 'emotional labour' varies both between and within organisations. In general, organisational culture favours the detached objective expert, who is the exemplar of bureaucratic rationality (Wajcman, 1999: 109). However, this culture operates differently for men and women. As Wajcman (1999) found in her study of the culture of large organisations, women and men in management are confronted with different behavioural expectations, and different interpretations are placed on their leadership styles, even though they may involve apparently identical modes of behaviour. That is, different 'emotional regimes' operate in the day-to-day workings of organisations, which generally work to men's advantage. For example, the expectation within organisations, that work would be separated from family life, favoured male managers. Women in senior management tended not to have children, whereas the male managers, who had partner-carers at home, did. Further, male managers tended to view women managers in a family role, expecting that they would offer emotional support as they might with their wives (Wajcman, 1999: 123). Other occupations with a preponderance of men – the skilled trades and the process, plant and machine operative jobs – exhibit a similarly gendered culture, though with different manifestations. Although a growing number of women are moving into some of these fields, expectations about the separation of work and family life and the assumption that women are the 'natural' carers in the home, as well as long-entrenched views about men's and women's different abilities to undertake certain tasks, again tend to disadvantage women. Policies and practices reflect and reinforce this division of labour. For example, hiring practices sometimes exclude women (but not men) of child-bearing age from exposure to toxic chemicals which may reduce women's access to certain jobs. Protective labour legislation in some jurisdictions (e.g. the US, from 1874 until 1964) has often prevented women from holding jobs requiring heavy lifting, long hours, or night work (Spain, 1992: 202).

The valuing of 'emotional labour' in the growing service sector demands that education and training systems produce workers with requisite skills in 'emotional management'. That is, they need to learn the rules for how they feel (i.e. 'feeling rules' [Hochschild, 1983] or 'display rules' [Goleman, 1995]) and to know how to inter-pret those rules (know what they *should* feel) in different contexts. According to Goleman (1995) and others, one of the major goals of 'emotional literacy' is to school people in these rules so that the expression of appropriate emotions becomes a straightforward matter. By practicing how to control one's responses to encounters that are not stressful, appropriate responses will become *automatic* when one is under stress (Goleman, 1995: 147). That is, they are required to undertake 'deep acting' (Hochschild, 1983: 35). Part of learning these rules is learning the *economy of affect*; that is, learning when to be economical in one's expenditure of 'emotional labour' (see McElhinny,

1994: 165). For many jobs and in many situations, 'surface acting' rather then 'deep acting' is called for. Police officers, and other workers, who are dealing with difficult, violent, or potentially 'emotionally taxing' situations, choose carefully the situations in which they express positive affect – as though they are on a limited budget (McElhinny, 1994: 165). Too much expression of positive affect in some jobs and certain situations is seen to detrimentally affect one's performance.

As Hochschild indicates, a language of rights and duties often pervades discussions about feelings; for example, one may speak of 'having the right' to feel angry at someone or chide oneself or others for not having expressed one's feelings as one *should* (see Hochschild, 2003: 97).

> Rights and duties set out the properties as to the *extent* (one can feel 'too' angry or 'not angry enough'), the *direction* (one can feel sad when one should feel happy), and the *duration* of a feeling, given the situation against which it is set. These rights and duties of feeling are a clue to the depth of social convention, to one final reach of social control. (Hochschild, 2003: 97)

Although Hochschild does not say as much, the language of rights and duties is the language of citizenship, which can be either inclusive or exclusive, depending upon one's ability or preparedness to sub-scribe to emotional imperatives. Following Hochschild, if one can-not or does not express emotion in prescribed ways (i.e. to the 'right' extent, direction, and duration), one is liable to be ostracised or denied access to certain kinds of work or activity. Since rights usually imply duties or obligations, the right to 'be emotional' means that one is generally presumed to have a duty to deal with the consequences of expressing one's feelings, including 'sharing feelings' with others in some cases. This can make one vulnerable to the policing of one's emotions by others. The focus on 'emotional literacy', above, involving 'opening up' or 'getting in touch' with one's emotions so that one may utilise those feelings beneficially, indeed, implies some degree of scrutiny by others, particularly psychologists, psychiatrists, social workers, and so on. The failure to demonstrate such 'emotional management' carries the danger of censure, ostracism, or 'treatment'.

As Hochschild notes, 'feeling rules' are gendered: men and women learn to express emotion in certain prescribed gender-typical ways. In becoming 'competent' citizens, men and women come to know what is 'right' for them to feel in certain jobs or certain situations, including those feelings which are gender-specific. For example, the bride will have a prior notion of what feelings are 'feelable', which is derived from the 'collectively shared emotional vocabulary' (Hochschild, 2003: 121). The display of positive affect can be seen as one of the 'privileges' of secretaries, one of their chief sources of power and one of the few avenues to professional advancement, especially when loyalty and care for a particular boss can lead to promotion when that boss is promoted (McElhinny, 1994: 163). The assumption that women are 'more in touch' with their feelings or that caring comes 'naturally' means that women are seen as especially well equipped for many jobs and activities in the service economy. That is, women's 'emotional labour' is potentially more exploitable in the service-based economy than is men's. Notwithstanding emergent archetypes of the 'new man', who is more 'in touch' with his emotions, men tend to be seen as 'the less emotional sex' and hence less 'naturally' inclined to care for or serve others. Consequently, they are seen as in need of more preparatory or on-the-job training in the 'emotional management' required in the growing service sector. Popular cultural images of emotionally weak or openly aggressive men reinforce the perception that men are especially in need of 'emotional literacy'. Because women are seen, in the main, to have more emotional resources, it happens that it is they who are most likely to be called upon to offer help to the emotionally lacking male, in their roles as partners, parents, or professionals.

From what has been said it should be clear that the recent emphasis on 'emotional literacy', particularly of men and boys, serves to divert attention from the substantial economic, social, and political issues at stake in the definition of problems as having an 'emotional' basis. The focus on 'emotional deficits' and the educative and training needs of the 'emotionally illiterate' obscures the politics of gender which operates at the level of discourse and language (dominant gender–emotion associations, which posit women as 'the more emotional sex') as well as in everyday practices (of employment, and the strict demarcation of work life and home life). Mirroring the division of physical labour in society, the division of emotional labour is deeply gendered, with women undertaking the overwhelming proportion of 'emotional labour'. Such a division serves to keep women in low paid, poorly compensated sectors of the economy and renders invisible their unpaid or poorly paid contributions to society. It also contributes to the de-valuing of certain categories of work with a high 'emotional labour' content, particularly unpaid caring work, and voluntary service work in the community. Finally, it operates to limit men's experiences and opportunities, by restricting their paid and unpaid labours to certain gender-typical activities. Challenging gender-typical constructions of emotional labour is therefore integral to changing the gender division of labour as a whole. Unfortunately, the way questions are currently posed about gender and emotion limit what are seen to be the possibilities of change. In particular, the operation of dualistic thought, whereby the world is viewed in terms of oppositions – men/women, subject/object, nature/culture, emotion/ reason – constrains both theoretical understanding and practice in relation to gender and emotion. In the effort to develop new ways of thinking about and 'enacting' gender, it is important to identify how established categories and dualisms constrain thought.

'Nature', 'nurture' and 'difference'

As noted in Chapter 1, debates about gender differences in emotionality, like those in many other areas of discourse about 'difference', have been dominated by a discourse about the relative contributions of 'nature' and 'nurture' to human identity and action. The significance of the 'nature versus nurture' debate in discussions about gender and emotion has been referred to at various points in previous chapters. On the side of 'nurture' are those who argue that differences between men and women are due to different socialising pressures, with girls being offered more scope to develop their emotional side. However, proponents of this argument not always explain why these pressures operate differently for boys and girls. On the 'nature' side are those who contend that differences are 'hard-wired'; that is, men and women have different genetic make-ups or have differently wired brains. The frequent implication here is that 'biology is destiny'; that 'nature' determines 'who we are' and how we act and limits prospects for change. Those who side with 'nature', including some feminists (see, e.g. Badinter, 1995; Christen, 1991), tend to equate biological 'sex' with social 'gender': 'who we are' and how we act depends on whether our genetic make-up is XY or XX. In relation to the 'nurture' position, the psychoanalytic framework, and specifically the 'object-relations' version proposed by Gilligan (1982) in her analysis of sex differences in morality, has been highly influential. From this perspective, early childhood experiences within the family are crucial in the moulding of identity. During their early development, girls maintain strong relationships with their mothers and consequently see themselves as part of a network of relationships, whereas boys attain their identity by separating early from their mother and becoming autonomous. Implicit in the quote from Kindlon and Thompson (1999), referred to earlier in this Chapter, is the psycho-analytic idea that the emotional life of boys is stifled through competition with their (often absent) fathers. The need for men to emotionally 'reconnect' with their fathers has been a recurrent theme in a number of popular writings on men.

As mentioned in Chapters 1 and 2, arguments about the 'natural', particularly genetic, basis of emotional and other differences between men and women have a long history, however, more and more, reference has been made to neuroscience theories of brain wiring. These theories suggest that there is less scope for changing the way men think or respond, since the hormonal environments individuals experienced while they were still foetuses in their mothers' wombs configures the brain for masculine or feminine traits or behaviours at an early development stage (see, e.g. Pease and Pease, 2001: 57). Although a growing number of writers have acknowledged some contribution from both 'nature' and 'nurture', there has been a tendency for writers to favour one influence over the other. Not sur-prisingly, given the division of knowledge and intellectual labour, natural scientists tend to favour 'nature', while social scientists generally favour 'nurture'. Regardless of emphasis, however, most writers fail to appreciate the historical and social production of 'biology' and of the dichotomy of 'nature/nurture'. This reflects an unshakeable faith in the ability of science to resolve a question that is a matter of values and politics.

Social values and political influences have shaped the framing of the 'nature/nurture' debate through its history. During the post-Second World War period there have been shifts in the relative emphasis ascribed 'nature' and 'nurture' in social explanation in response to social and political contexts: first, away from the former towards the latter (against a background of fears about resurgent eugenics) and, second, a reverse of this balance towards the end of the twentieth century (Rheinberger, 1995: 257). 'Second-wave' feminists, for example, had been successful in the late 1960s and 1970s in shaping debates about the influence of 'culture' on the formation of 'gender' in their efforts to challenge the notion of 'biology-as-destiny' (i.e. sex differences). Many policies developed since then, for example equal opportunities, have their origins in feminist agitations during this period. Recently, however, the dichotomy of 'nature/nurture' (or, alternatively, 'biology/society') has come into question (Rheinberger, 1995). The debate over 'nature' versus 'nurture' in debates about gender and emotion suggests that a clear boundary can be drawn between the natural and the social, between facts and values, and subjectivity and objectivity. Increasingly, sciences' claim to provide an objective, factual understanding of nature has been substantially challenged. The rhetoric of naturalism denies the power relations of science and scientific knowledge. In research on sex and gender, 'nature' has been used to provide legitimacy for a particular point of view (Tiefer, 1998). Tiefer shows how, in the history of sex research, the employment of concepts such as 'sexual behaviour' was shaped by prevailing views on 'normal' sexuality and the need for researchers to gain the endorsement of powerful interests (e.g. research funders, such as Rockefeller) (1998: 157–160). For example, Masters and Johnsons' influential study on the physiology of male and female sexual response which suggests a natural 'human sexual response cycle', involving an invariant sequence of four phases of physical changes occurring throughout the body when a person was sexually aroused, reveals a bias towards a orgasm-oriented sexual pattern that they already assumed was normal and universal (Tiefer, 1998: 163–166). Even among more critical scholars there is often an apparent blindness to the biases and values which underpin science, and specifically scientific views on sex/gender. Few scholars have asked why, in studies of men's and women's experiences, conduct, and physical and mental make-ups, there is a focus on difference rather than similarity. Science is a social product and scientific knowledge inevitably reflects the values and beliefs of the society in which it arises. Portrayals of 'nature' are shaped by 'culture', and vice versa. Scientific theories of genetic-based difference and behaviour, for example, reflect ideas about 'normal' identity and social relations. Research into the so-called 'gay gene', and subsequent media reports and public responses, illustrate how assumptions about the natural and the normal may shape the conduct of research, and the interpretation and portrayal of findings (Petersen, 1999). If prevailing constructions of gender and emotion are to be challenged, science's assumptions and representations need to be exposed and their sociopolitical implications spelt out.

Science and the study of gender and emotion

In contemporary societies, the scientific worldview is generally more highly valued and seen as more authoritative than other ways of knowing. Science defines what is taken for granted in the daily lives and activities of literally billions of people (Fox, 1999: 442). Knowledge based on experience or immersion in contexts (what some people describe as 'intuitive' knowledge) has comparatively low status compared with the abstract and systematic theory and rationality of science (see Flyvbjerg, 2001). Central to the self-representation of science is the view that rational objective knowledge and science fact can, and should be, separate from 'emotional' (i.e. irrational) influence and that science fact can be easily separated from science fiction. As in other areas of contemporary life, in science, the 'emotions' are seen as potentially disruptive. Thus, natural scientists and many social scientists who study 'emotion' and 'gender differences in emotion', as in other areas of science and social science, aim to gain 'dispassionate knowledge'. Through the adoption of various 'controls', they aim to screen out any subjective influences. However, subjectivity and value biases inevitably make their appearances in the research process, in the questions asked, in the selection of variables, in the analysis of data, in the choice of language, and in the communication of findings. For example, in studying the topic of aggression, psychologists have come to their work with the evolutionist assumption that parallels can be drawn between human behaviour and other animal behaviour and that certain observed recurrent behaviours are 'adaptive' (see Chapter 2). The language of competition within evolutionary theory imports cultural norms into the field of explanation. Further, as feminist historians and philosophers of science have argued, scientific knowledge has a *masculine* bias (see, e.g. Haraway, 1990, 1991, 1997; Harding, 1986, 1991; Keller, 1992; Steinberg, 1997). That is, scientific knowledge reflects the standpoint of the male scientists who produce most of the knowledge as well as the values and priorities of a masculine culture. Inherent in masculine culture is a focus on difference (particularly natural difference), hierarchy, and dualism. Cultural stereotypes of gender differences, and beliefs about the 'naturalness' of gendered divisions of labour, shape scientific explanations, for example the theory of 'brain sex' (see Vines, 1993: 85–123). These stereotypes and beliefs, which circulate in the broader culture, are reproduced through the practices of research, including the selection of topics and the categories of analysis.

As Tavris (1998) argues, research on biologically based differences between men and women is inherently more attractive to researchers, the media, and powerful groups than research on sex similarities. Drug companies benefit from the medicalising of psychological problems and the promotion of drug treatments, and have been known to stifle research, non-medical explanations, and treatments of mood disorders, 'PMS', and sexual dysfunction (Tavris, 1998: 17). As Tavris puts it,

> Researchers profit from biological approaches to gender differences because there is more money, fame, and glamour in doing MRI [magnetic resonance imaging] studies than in doing historical, cultural, and sociological studies. Conservatives profit from theories of women's 'natural' nurturance and men's 'natural' competitiveness, for these ideas support their traditional philosophy that men belong at work and mothers belong in the home. Those in power profit from theories that women are naturally more relational and cooperative, naturally averse to exercising power, because then women who are autonomous, ambitious, and powerful can be excoriated as being 'unnatural'. (Tavris, 1998: 17)

Critical social science can play a crucial role in showing how scientific research helps construct 'truth' about the relationship between gender and emotion, and how the research process is shaped by economic and political interests. It is important to show how the categories and objects of science change through time and vary across contexts and in response to changing configurations of power and knowledge. Historical and ethnographic methods can highlight the contingency of the dominant ways of knowing and how research may be used to fabricate identities (e.g. the 'emotionally deficient' boy or man) and legitimise certain policies and practices (e.g. 'emotional literacy' programmes). The particular historical approach proposed by Nietzsche, and developed by Foucault, namely genealogy, has significant potential in this regard, having found application previously, in studies of surveillance medicine (Armstrong, 1995), the problem of child mental health (Tyler, 1997), and 'multiple personality disorder' (Hacking, 1995). Foucault advocated historical investigation as a tool for 'diagnosing the present'; that is, for making the present strange, rather than the past familiar. The explicit goal of genealogical work is to disturb certainties and taken-for-granted categories such as 'boys' and 'girls' as pre-given objects of study about which science produces more or less adequate accounts (Tyler, 1997: 78). As Flyvbjerg explains,

> Genealogy takes as its objects exactly those institutions and practices which, like rationality, are usually thought to be excluded from change. It tries to show the way in which they, too, undergo changes as a result of historical developments; and it also tries to demonstrate how such changes escape our notice, how it is often in the interest of those institutions and practices to mask their specific genealogy and historical character. Genealogy therefore has direct practical, often political, implications. By demonstrating the contingent character of those institutions and practices that traditional history exhibits as unchanging, genealogy creates the possibility of altering them. (Flyvbjerg, 2001: 115)

In relation to the analysis of gender and emotion specifically, genealogical methods can help reveal how scientific fields of study such as sociobiology, evolutionary psychology, and neuroscience fabricate identities and difference and how they may serve to legitimise practices such as men's violence against women (see Chapter 3). My analysis of the history of the psychology of aggression revealed continuities in assumptions about innate sex differences in diverse theories (see Chapter 2). Historical deconstructive work has proved useful in studies of the construction of sex differences in anatomy (e.g. Moore and Clarke, 1995, 2001; Schiebinger, 1986, 1990), the 'discovery' of hormones (Oudshoorn, 1994) and the rise of sexual science (Bland and Doan, 1998a,b; Russett, 1989), and has significant potential in the study of gender and emotion, which has thus far been dominated by the perspectives of biology, psychology, and psychoanalysis.

The media and the portrayal of gender and emotion

As I argued in Chapters 3 and 4, the media in its diverse forms, including the print news media, the broadcast media, advertising, the Internet, and magazines and other popular outlets, is likely to play a key role in shaping public discourse about gender differences in emotion. It is crucial then for critical scholars to expose the representational practices of media and explore their political implications. The media 'framing' of issues can serve to privilege certain voices and viewpoints and silence others (Miller and Riechert, 2000), and amplify risk and generate anxiety by giving undue prominence to certain aspects of issues (Murdock, *et al.*, 2003). For the public, the media in its various forms, is likely to be a major source for scientific knowledge, such as in the fields of medical and behavioural genetics – which tend to provide a reductionist view of the human body, behaviour, and difference (see Petersen, 2001). The media portrayal of gender–emotion associations has been referred to at various points in this book. In Chapter 3, I showed how news portrayals of the 2003 Gulf War serve to 'normalise' the links between masculinity, aggression, and war. Both news stories and accompanying illustrative material of combat situations convey the view that men are the 'more active sex' and inherently aggressive and that war is 'men's business', while offering little insight into the lives and experiences of the substantial number of women who were involved in various significant 'behind-the-scenes', particularly support, roles. It was suggested that the portrayal of gender during the war mirrors the gendered hierarchies within news production. Women's voices and roles in war remain largely invisible or passive, for example, as victims of war. As was evident during the 2003 Gulf War, there may be a close interdependence between the institutions of the military and the institutions of the media that make it difficult to challenge the media's representational practices in relation to aggression, war, and gender. The 'embedding' of the media among combat units resulted in tight control over media reporting and images. Although the analysis was limited to war reporting, and specifically the 2003 Gulf War, one can point to parallels from other areas of media use and representation for insight into how the practices of the media may shape and limit public discourse about gender and emotion. These include portrayals of romance and popular advice for women, for example in relation to meeting the opposite sex (see Chapter 4).

Media portrayals of discrete issues such as acts of familicide (murder-suicides) by possessive husbands, women's responses to public issues (e.g. war), or men's involvement in childcare, contribute to forging cultural associations between gender and particular kinds of emotional experience and expression. Examples of such media portrayals are numerous, but some recent ones are worth mentioning. The highly publicised resignation of UK's education secretary, Estelle Morris, in October 2002, on the grounds that 'she was incapable of providing the right strategic management to run a big government department' offers a particularly clear illustration of how gender and emotion may be linked in the news media. The issue was especially 'newsworthy' because it involved a female politician and it involved public disclosure about the unwritten 'rules of feeling' that apply to (mostly male) politicians. The announcement of the resignation gave rise to extensive public debate about the acceptability of politicians expressing a weakness in the public domain. Whereas male politicians would be expected to 'tough it out', the Minister confessed to 'not being up to the job'. As she was quoted, 'I was not good at dealing with the modern media. I have not done the job as well as I should have done' (Wintour and Watt, 2002: 1). In a second article, in the same edition of this newspaper, which referred to a recent 'A-level debate', some clarification is offered: 'She was frustrated...that the rules of the game of politics had prevented her from making clear the strength of her concern and sympathy for the students involved. Politics, she lamented, did not permit its practitioners to say sorry, for fear of being accused of weakness – particularly risky in a woman' (Ward and Smithers, 2002: 3). In effect, her 'failure', portrayed here, was not displaying the archetypal masculine emotional characteristics expected of political incumbents. Women who do not learn or are not willing to play according to the male-coded rules are vulnerable to the charge of 'not being up to the job'. Periodic cases of women killing partners or killing their children also tend to receive prominent news coverage, because this is seen as 'against women's nature'. For example, an article, 'Mother accused of killing babies' opens with, 'A mother defied nature and instinct to murder two of her babies as they lay in their cots, a Winchester crown court heard yesterday...'. The article went on to cite the prosecution argument that, 'For a mother to attack her own child in this way is of course against nature and instinct, but the prosecution say the evidence will demonstrate that this is what Angela Cannings has done' (Hall, 2002: 5).

The prominence given by the media to cases of male partners undertaking a major role in childcare, while seeming to challenge gender stereotypes by offering an archetype of the 'new man', confirm that such a role is out of the ordinary and hence 'newsworthy'. One article referred to some instances where 'high profile fathers' left work, or changed their working hours, to take a greater role in childcare (Larner, 2003: 12). One father, a 'chief executive of one of Britain's biggest insurance companies', was said to have 'resign[ed] from his £340,000-a-year job after only seven weeks to spend more time with his nine-year-old triplets'. Such experiences are presented as a personal sacrifice and a struggle, suggesting that women who routinely undertake this role do not suffer a similar experience because it is 'natural' for them. For example, the feelings of one father (Paul Maynard, a 'proud "home-dad" to six children' who 'made a decision to leave his job in a bank eight years ago and has not looked back since') are recounted:

> Mr Maynard says he doesn't feel the family has suffered financially but admits to struggling against years of male conditioning: 'Deep down you feel an in-built need to have a career and bring in a wage to support the family. I've tried to suppress it, but it's still there.' (Larner, 2003: 12)

Another article on men and childcare offers a play on the stereotype of masculinity by asking, in its headline, 'Are you tough enough?' It notes that, 'Poor pay, gruelling work... the biggest job challenge for men today is down at the nursery. And that means kids not plants...' (Roberts, 2003: 17). The article goes on to note that for those working in full-time childcare the wages are low ('begin[ning] at below £4,000 a year and reach only £13–15,000 for a nursery manager, working very long hours. Women can earn more stacking shelves in Asda...'). The subtext here is that those men who undertake such care are extraordinarily selfless, and somehow offering a greater sacrifice than women. While the article does offer some analysis – it goes on to cite research on 'deeply embedded' gender differences in the running of nurseries and that 'To recruit more men childcare providers will have to provide positive images, a shake-up in training, a change among careers advisors...and a hike in pay...' – the fact that men's involvement in childcare is 'newsworthy' at all evidently does not warrant comment. Significantly, another article, *New dads get raw deal from bosses*, documents the substantial difficulties confronting fathers who wish to spend more time caring for their children, and their fears about damaging their careers. Referring to the findings of a recent report by Work Foundation on unpaid childcare leave, the article notes that 'Men are resorting to "stealth parenting" – spending more time with their children, but inventing business meetings to cover absences from the office – for fear that admitting to childcare responsibilities damages their careers' (Hinsliff, 2002a: 1). Given the media's focus on the exceptional, sensational, and human interest aspect of issues, the above portrayals are hardly surprising. Only when men's involvement in care reaches a point where it ceases to be out of the ordinary, and hence non-'newsworthy', can it be assumed that real change in gender definitions and roles has taken place.

The law and the regulation of gender and emotion

A substantial body of feminist literature has highlighted the male gender bias of law, which operates at a number of levels. A certain style of reasoning associated with masculinity is valued, while a particular gender division of emotional and physical labour is taken as given. The criminal justice system clearly displays a number of 'man-made' features: the system has been designed to control and rehabilitate men and decisions and policies are made predominantly by men (e.g. Arnot and Usborne, 1999; Heidenhohn, 1996; Kennedy, 1992; Naffine, 1987, 1995). Critical studies can help reveal how law and legal assumptions and processes, as well as the reporting of crime news, mirror and reinforce views on inherent gender differences in emotionality. As the feminist criminologist, Naffine (1987) has argued, law has a gender bias in the legal concept of the 'reasonable man' which provides the objective standard of human conduct. This concept, although avowedly gender neutral, is based on an assumed male subject and the characters used to illustrate the concept are invariably men (1987: 4). In cases of provocation, which is a defence to murder, for example, the legal standards are constructed from a male perspective and with men in mind, which means that women have difficulty fulfilling the criteria. The question for a jury in instances where provocation is raised is whether a 'reasonable man' might have suffered a temporary and sudden loss of self-control so that he was no longer 'master of his own mind' in circumstances like those described in tendered evidence (Kennedy, 1992: 200). As Helena Kennedy, a criminal justice lawyer, explains,

> Little account is taken of the cultural differences between men and women and the way that our socialisation affects our responses. Women are much less likely to respond to provocation immediately, for obvious physical and psychological reasons, and therefore self-defence and provocation are less available to them. But the legal standards are built upon ideas of instant ignition and a hotheaded rush to action. The spark has to be immediate, an assault which requires self-protection or a blow, a curse, an insult that goes to the core of a man's being. Judges try to create a parallel analogy, the trigger to violent reaction being terrible insults against a woman's chastity or her way of life, both of which are male ideas of what might make a woman run amok. (Kennedy, 1992: 200)

The legal concept of the 'reasonable man' has informed criminology, for example in the influential strain theory, where criminality is seen to arise from frustrated aspirations which are typically those defined by the standards of the successful middle-class male; that is, autonomy, ambition, and restraint in one's emotions (Naffine, 1987: 8–25). In general, women have been seen as more passive and law-abiding and, in cases where women do offend, their behaviour tends to be met with greater censure than that which applies to men committing a similar offence. As Kennedy observes, such gender biases operate on both sides of the bench. Women who commit crime are portrayed as a rare species (Kennedy, 1992: 20), while women who perform criminal advocacy are expected to assume a passive role and any aggression is viewed as 'phallic, certainly unattractive in a woman' (1992: 49).

In the UK, the Fawcett Society, an organisation which campaigns for equality between women and men in the UK, has made a considerable contribution to exposing the gender biases in law. In its final report, Commission on Women and the Criminal Justice System, launched in March 2004, the Society highlighted how the 'man-made' justice system frequently 'fails women' (http://www.fawcettsociety. org.uk). The Report, claimed to be 'the first of its kind internationally to look at women's experience right across the criminal justice system', presented evidence of poor conviction rates for rape and domestic violence, a massive (194 per cent) increase in the female prison rate over the last ten years, and a very poor representation of women in 'top jobs across the system' (e.g. the House of Lords, Chief Constables, Chief Officers of Probation, Chief Crown Prosecutors, and Prison Governors). It was noted that 'Sentences are getting harsher and the number of women in prison has risen dramatically – at a much faster rate than imprisonment of men – even though there has been no equivalent rise in female offending' (http://www.fawcettsociety. org.uk).

According to one interpretation, this trend of harsher sentences can be explained by the fact that 'the courts are losing sympathy with female defendants as the traditional perception dissipates of women being gentler and more law-abiding (Hinsliff, 2002b: 16). However, the Report noted that a range of factors may be relevant, including 'the inherent male bias in sentencing, the tendency to remand women in custody and the increase in women's offending especially in drug-related crimes'. (The Report noted that social exclusion and experiences of economic and social deprivation, which 'lie beyond the control mechanism of the criminal justice system', played a role in women's offending [http://www.fawcettsociety. org.uk].)

Although contributions such as those of the Fawcett Society have highlighted entrenched male biases in law, it would be wrong to suggest that there is little scope for change. Cross-cultural and historical work has revealed how laws may be manipulated by those subject to them in order to develop alternative models of gender relations that differ significantly from established norms. While legal systems may reflect and reinforce stereotype conceptions of femininity, women are by no means passive when it comes to fighting for their rights (Arnot and Usborne, 1999: 29). In arguing for a fairer legal system, feminists and other critical scholars need to not only expose how assumptions about difference, including difference in emotional make-up, work to disadvantage women, but also to explore how legal systems and legal categories and arguments may be exploited to create less gender-biased social arrangements.

A final word: 'emotion' in gender studies

Over the last three decades, the field of gender studies has produced a rich and varied literature, with contributions from many disciplines. The diversity and fragmentation of work is such there is often disagreement about even fundamental categories such as 'experience' and 'woman' and on the significance of distinctions such as 'sex' and 'gender' (see, e.g. Evans, 1997; Grant, 1993). Such diversity and fragmentation makes it difficult and hazardous to generalise about themes. If one can identify a broad unifying strand within this diversity it would have to be agreement on the significance of 'the body', its representation and/or its materiality, for defining difference and regulating relations between women and men. The contributions of writers such as Butler (1993), Bordo (1993), and Connell (1995) on gender and the body have helped recast thinking about the power relations of gender, and have inaugurated novel lines of enquiry. Approaches to 'the body', however, are themselves diverse, with theories of modernity vying with theories of postmodernity, which offer very different accounts of the materiality, stability and change-ability of the body and of supportive power relations. In comparison to research and writing on the significance of the body for gender, social science work on emotion and gender is underdeveloped. Insofar as 'emotion' is studied at all, it tends to be seen as an aspect of 'embodied' experience, and thus reducible to biology. The psycho-logical and psychoanalytic perspectives which dominate much thinking on emotion and gender reinforce this reductionism. The role of 'emotion' in the regulation of identity and of populations has thus far been largely overlooked. This relative neglect of 'emotion' in gender studies has inadvertently reinforced the mind–body dualism. That is, matters of the body are seen as somehow more significant than, and thus privileged over, matters of the mind and heart in understanding constructions and enactments of gender. This relative blindness, in gender studies, to 'emotion' and its politics can be seen as an artefact of the theoretical frameworks applied to the field of analysis. The cultural valuing of science (and of particular approaches) over other ways of knowing has resulted in certain biases being imported into social enquiries. As noted, above, the scientific study of emotion both mirrors and reinforces dualistic thought and the predominance of rationality over emotionality.

With recent changes in politics and power, and the emergence of new forms of governance focusing on the autonomous subject of choice and self-identity (Rose, 1999), there is an urgent need for gender scholars to take seriously the significance of 'emotion' for defining difference and regulating relations between men and women. In particular, it is important to explore how assumptions about gender differences in emotional experience and expression are used to explain patterns of inequality and to legitimate policies and practices in various domains of social life. Although feminists and masculinity scholars have long acknowledged the cultural links between emotionality and femininity and rationality and masculinity, they have tended to overlook the ways in which particular gender–emotion associations may mesh with broader governmental objectives. There has been little appreciation of how the very frameworks of understanding applied to the field of emotions, as developed by the 'psy' knowledges of human subjects (e.g. psychology, psychoanalysis, psychiatry), biology, and, increasingly, the neurosciences, serve to bring the regulation of subjectivity in line with dominant rationalities of rule. Just as there are many different approaches to 'the body', there are potentially many ways to view and analyse 'emotion' each with their own implied strategies for change. New theoretical approaches are urgently needed to understand how gender and emotion are linked in various social domains at different times and to help identify the opportunities for constructing and 'doing' gender differently. It is important to acknowledge the significance of the 'embodied' expression of emotion – for example, 'acting from the heart' – without resorting to biological explanations. New ways of thinking about gender and emotion and imaginative strategies for change are already being developed outside academe, often in response to pressing policy and practical issues, such as men's violence to women. For example, innovative approaches developed by Save the Children UK and NIKK, the Nordic Institute for Women's Studies and Gender Research, for addressing men's violence and HIV/AIDS prevention, respectively, and involving work with boys and girls in different countries, have shown how a multi-pronged approach focusing on the gender system may help change gender relations and reduce inequality (see Lewis, 2002; Thomson, 2002). Recent sociological interest in the emotions (e.g. Barbalet, 1998, 2002; Bendelow and Williams, 1998; Crawford, *et al.*, 1992; Hochschild, 1983, 2003) has served to highlight the significance of emotions in social life, but work is often overly abstract and disconnected from 'real world' issues. However, sociology offers useful tools for analysing 'emotion' and the construction and enactment of gender in specific domains (e.g. male-to-female violence and sexual exploitation), and can assist in the effort to rethink basic concepts (e.g. 'experience', 'woman', 'man') and distinctions (e.g. 'difference' versus 'sameness') that have been central to gender studies (see Young, 1990). In particular, there is a need to acknowledge the political and ethical dimension of emotional life which is often neglected in sociological studies. The role of the emotions in governance – in how we are governed and in how we govern and conduct ourselves – needs more systematic attention. There is an urgent need for novel approaches and method-ologies for understanding the politics of gender–emotion associations. A more critical and historically informed analysis of gender and emotion can help reveal how 'emotion' may be constructed differ-ently for men and women and thereby assist us in seeing that there is nothing 'natural' or inevitable about current ways of being.

References

Aldridge, A. (2003) *Consumption*. Polity: Cambridge.

Allen, G. (1996) 'Science misapplied: the eugenic age revisited', *Technology Review*, August/September: 23–31.

Allen, G. (1999) 'Modern biological determinism: the violence initiative, the human genome project, and the new eugenics', in M. Fortun and E. Mendelsohn (eds) *The Practices of Human Genetics*. Kluwer Academic Publishers: Dordrecht.

Armstrong, D. (1995) 'The rise of surveillance medicine', *Sociology of Health and Illness*, 17: 393–404.

Arnot, M. L. and Usborne, C. (1999) 'Why gender and crime? Aspects of an international debate', in M. L. Arnot and C. Usborne (eds) *Gender and Crime in Modern Europe*. UCL Press: London.

Badinter, E. (1995) *XY: On Masculine Identity*. Columbia University Press: New York.

Bandura, A. (1977) *Social Learning Theory*. Prentice-Hall: Englewood Cliffs, NJ.

Bandura, A. and Walters, R. H. (1963) *Social Learning and Personality Development*, Holt, Rinehart and Winston: New York.

Barbalet, J. (1998) *Emotion, Social Theory, and Social Structure: A Macrosociological Approach*. Cambridge University Press: Cambridge.

Barbalet, J. (ed.) (2002) *Emotions and Sociology*. Blackwell Publishing/The Sociological Review: Oxford.

Baron-Cohen, S. (2003) *The Essential Difference: Men, Women and the Extreme Male Brain*. Allen Lane: London.

Barry, K. (1979) *Female Sexual Slavery*. New York University Press: New York and London.

Baudrillard, J. (1995) *The Gulf War did not Take Place*. Power Publications: Sydney.

Bauman, Z. (2003) *Liquid Love: On the Frailty of Human Bonds*. Polity: Cambridge.

Beck, U. and Beck-Gernsheim, E. (1995) *The Normal Chaos of Love*. Polity Press: Cambridge.

Bendelow, G. (2000) *Pain and Gender*. Pearson Education Ltd: Harlow.

Bendelow, G. and Williams, S. (ed.) (1998) *Emotions in Social Life: Critical Themes and Contemporary Issues*. Routledge: London and New York.

Benjamin, J. and Rabinbach, A. (1989) 'Forward', in K. Theweleit (ed.) *Male Fantasies*, Volume 2: *Male Bodies: Psychoanalyzing the White Terror*. Polity Press: Cambridge.

Ben-Ze'ev, A. (2004) *Love Online: Emotions on the Internet*. Cambridge University Press: Cambridge.

Berkowitz, L. (1993) *Aggression: Its Causes, Consequences and Control*. McGraw-Hill: New York.

Bickford, A. (2003) 'The militarization of masculinity in the former German Democratic Republic', in P. R. Higate (ed.) *Military Masculinities: Identity and the State*. Praeger: Westport, Connecticut and London.

Bittman, M. and Pixley, J. (1997) *The Double Life of the Family: Myth, Hope and Experience*. Allen & Unwin: St Leonards.

Bjorkqvist, K. (1994) 'Sex differences in physical, verbal, and indirect aggression: a review of recent research', *Sex Roles*, 30, 3/4: 177–188.

Bjorkqvist, K. and Niemela, P. (1992) *Of Mice and Men: Aspects of Female Aggression*. Academic Press: San Diego.

Bland, L. and Doan, L. (1998a) *Sexology Uncensored: The Documents of Sexual Science*. Polity Press: Cambridge.

Bland, L. and Doan, L. (1998b) *Sexology in Culture: Labelling Bodies and Desires*. Polity Press: Cambridge.

Bleier, R. (1984) *Science and Gender: A Critique of Biology and its Theories on Women*. Pergamon Press: New York.

Bly, R. (1990) *Iron John: A Book About Men*. Addison-Wesley: Reading, MA.

Bordo, S. (1993) *Unbearable Weight: Feminism, Western Culture, and the Body*. University of California Press: Berkeley and Los Angeles.

Borger, J. and McCarthy, R. (2003) 'US troops gain foothold in heart of Baghdad', *The Guardian*, April 8, p. 1.

Bourke, J. (1999) *An Intimate History of Killing: Face-to-Face Killing in Twentieth-Century Warfare*. Granta Books: London.

Brody, L. R. and Hall, J. (1993) 'Gender and emotion', in M. Lewis and J. Haviland (eds) *Handbook of Emotion*. The Guilford Press: New York and London.

Bullough, V. L. (1994) *Science in the Bedroom: A History of Sex Research*. Basic Books: New York.

Burbank, V. (1994) 'Cross-cultural perspectives on aggression in women and girls: an introduction', *Sex Roles*, 30, 3/4: 169–188.

Burr, V. (1995) *An Introduction to Social Constructionism*. Routledge: London and New York.

Butler, J. (1990) *Gender Trouble: Feminism and the Subversion of Identity*. Routledge: New York.

Butler, J. (1993) *Bodies that Matter: On the Discursive Limits of 'Sex'*. Routledge: New York.

Campbell, A. (2002) *A Mind of Her Own: The Evolutionary Psychology of Women*. Oxford University Press: Oxford.

Canary, D. J. and Emmers-Sommer, T. M. (1997) *Sex and Gender Differences in Personal Relationships*. The Guildford Press: New York and London.

Cant, R. (1994) 'Just care-giving: whose work, whose control?' in C. Waddell and A. R. Petersen (eds) *Just Health: Inequality in Illness, Care and Prevention*. Churchill Livingstone: Melbourne.

Chodorow, N. (1978) *The Reproduction of Mothering*. The University of California Press: Berkeley.

Chodorow, N. (1999) *The Power of Feelings: Personal Meaning in Psychoanalysis, Gender, and Culture*. Yale University Press: New Haven and London.

Christen, Y. (1991) *Sex Differences: Modern Biology and the Unisex Fallacy*. Transaction Publishers: New Brunswick.

Ciarrochi, J., Forgas, J. P. and Mayer, J. D. (eds) (2001) *Emotional Intelligence in Everyday Life: A Scientific Inquiry*. Psychology Press: Philadelphia, PA.

Cohen, C. (1990) '"Clean bombs" and clean language', in J. B. Elshtain and S. Tobias (eds) *Women, Militarism and War: Essays in History, Politics and Social Theory*. Rowman and Littlefield: Savage, Maryland.

Cohen, C. (1993) 'Wars, wimps, and women: talking gender and thinking war', in M. Cooke and A. Woollacott (eds) *Gendering War Talk*. Princeton University Press: Princeton, NJ.

Connell, R. W. (1995) *Masculinities*. Allen & Unwin: Sydney.

Connell, R. W. (2000) *The Men and the Boys*. Polity Press: Cambridge.

Connolly, K. (2001) 'A wedding in Berlin for two beaming brides', *The Guardian*, 2 August, p. 16.

Conrad, P. and Schneider, J. W. (1992) *Deviance and Medicalization: From Badness to Sickness*. Expanded Edition. Temple University Press: Philadelphia.

Cooke, M. (1993) 'Wo-man, retelling the war myth', in M. Cooke and A. Woollacott (eds) *Gendering War Talk*. Princeton University Press: Princeton, NJ.

Cornelius, A. R. (1996) *The Science of Emotion: Research and Tradition in the Psychology of Emotion*. Prenctice-Hall: New Jersey.

Costin, L. B. (1982) 'Feminism, pacifism, internationalism and the 1915 International Congress of Women', *Women's Studies International Forum*, 5, 3/4: 301–315.

Court-Brown, W. M. (1967) *Human Population Cytogenetics*. Wiley: New York.

Cramer, D. (1998) *Close Relationships: The Study of Love and Friendship*. Arnold: London.

Crawford, J., Kippax, S., Onyx, J., Gault, U. and Benton, P. (1992) *Emotion and Gender: Constructing Meaning from Memory*. Sage: London.

Cruikshank, B. (1996) 'Revolutions within: self-government and self-esteem', in A. Barry, T. Osborne and N. Rose (eds) *Foucault and Political Reason: Liberalism, Neo-Liberalism and Rationalities of Government*. UCL Press: London.

Darwin, C. (1872) *Expression of the Emotions in Man and Animals*. John Murray: London.

Daston, L. (1996) 'The naturalized female intellect', in C. F. Graumann and K. J. Gergen (eds) *Historical Dimensions of Psychological Discourse*. Cambridge University Press: Cambridge.

David, D. S. and Brannon, R. (eds) (1976) *The Forty-nine Percent Majority: The Male Sex Role*. Addison-Wesley: Reading, MA.

De Cataldo Neuburger, L. and Valentini, T. (1996) *Women and Terrorism*. Macmillan Press Ltd: Houndmills.

De Pauw, L. G. (1998) *Battle Cries and Lullabies: Women in War from Prehistory to the Present*. University of Oklahoma Press: Norman.

deMause, L. (2002) *The Emotional Life of Nations*. Karnac: New York and London.

Dennett, D. C. (2003) *Freedom Evolves*. Allen Lane: London.

Denzin, N. K. (1984) *On Understanding Emotion*. Jossey-Bass Inc., Publishers: San Francisco, CA and London.

Department for Education and Skills (2003) *Developing Children's Social, Emotional and Behavioural Skills: Guidance*. DfES: London.

Deyo, Y. and Deyo, S. (2002) *Speed Dating: The Smarter, Faster Way to Lasting Love*. HarperCollins: New York.

Diamond, I. and Orenstein, G. F. (1990) *Reweaving the World: The Emergence of Ecofeminism*. Sierra Club Books: San Francisco.

Dimen, M. (1995) 'On "our nature": a prolegomenon to a relational theory of sexuality', in T. Domenici and R. C. Lesser (eds) *Disorienting Sexuality: Psychoanalytic Reappraisals of Sexual Identities*. Routledge: New York.

Dollard, J., Miller, N. E., Doob, L. W., Mowrer, O. H. and Sears, R. R. (1949; orig. 1939) *Frustration and Aggression*, 7th edition. Yale University Press: New Haven.

Dorsch, E., Livingstone, J. and Rankin, J. (1991) 'If patriarchy creates war, can feminism create peace?' in A. E. Hunter (ed.) *On Peace, War, and Gender: A Challenge to Biological Explanations*. The Feminist Press: New York.

Drever, J. (1917) *Instinct in Man: A Contribution to the Psychology of Education*. University Press: Cambridge.

Dubberley, E. (2004) 'Helping people click', Online, *The Guardian*, 22 January, pp. 26–27.

Duncombe, J. and Marsden, D. (1993) 'Love and Intimacy: The Gender Division of Emotion and "Emotion Work": A Neglected Aspect of Sociological Discussion of Heterosexual Relationships', *Sociology*, 27, 2: 221–241.

Duncombe, J. and Marsden, D. (1996) '"Workaholics" and "wingeing women": theorising intimacy and emotion work: the last frontier of gender inequality?', *The Sociological Review*, 43, 1: 150–169.

Duncombe, J. and Marsden, D. (1998) '"Stepford wives" and "hollow men"? Doing emotion work, doing gender and "authenticity" in intimate heterosexual relationships', in G. Bendelow and S. J. Williams (eds) *Emotions in Social Life: Critical Themes and Contemporary Issues*. Routledge: London and New York.

Duncombe, J. and Marsden, D. (2002) 'Whose orgasm is it anyway? "Sex work" in long-term heterosexual couple relationships', in S. Jackson and S. Scott (eds) *Gender: A Sociological Reader*. Routledge: London and New York.

Durban, E. F. M. and Bowlby, J. (1939) *Personal Aggressiveness and War*. Columbia University Press: New York.

Eagly, A. H. (1995) 'The science and politics of comparing women and men', *American Psychologist*, 50, 3: 145–158.

Editorial Staff (1981) *The Macquarie Dictionary*. Macquarie Library Pty Ltd: St Leonards.

Edley, N. and Wetherell, M. (1996) 'Masculinity, power and identity', in M. Mac an Ghaill (ed.) *Understanding Masculinities: Social Relations and Cultural Arenas*. Open University Press: Buckingham and Philadelphia.

Ehrenreich, B. (1997) *Blood Rites: Origins and History of the Passions of War*. Virago: London.

Ehrenreich, B. and English, D. (1979) *For Her Own Good: 150 Years of the Experts' Advice to Women*. Anchor Books: New York.

Ehrenreich, B. and Hochschild, A. R. (2002) *Global Woman: Nannies, Maids and Sex Workers in the New Economy*. Granta Books: London.

164   *References*

Elias, N. (1978) *The Civilizing Process: The History of Manners*. Urizon Books: New York.
Ellis, H. (1925) *Studies in the Psychology of Sex*, Volume 3: *Analysis of the Sexual Impulse, Love and Pain, The Sexual Impulse in Women*, 2nd edition. F. A. Davis and Company, Publishers: Philadelphia.
Enloe, C. H. (1994) 'The politics of constructing the American woman soldier', in E. Addis, V. E. Russo and L. Sebesta (eds) *Women Soldiers: Images and Realities*. St Martin's Press: New York.
Erickson, J. A. (with Steffen, S. A.) (1999) *Kiss and Tell: Surveying Sex in the Twentieth Century*. Harvard University Press: Cambridge, MA and London.
Evans, M. (1997) *Introducing Contemporary Feminist Thought*. Polity Press: Cambridge.
Evans, M. (2004) *Love: An Unromantic Discussion*. Polity: Cambridge.
Fausto-Stirling, A. (1992) *Myths of Gender: Biological Theories about Women and Men*. 2nd edition. Basic Books: New York.
Fausto-Stirling, A. (2000) 'Beyond difference: feminism and evolutionary psychology', in H. Rose and S. Rose (eds) *Alas, Poor Darwin: Arguments Against Evolutionary Psychology*. Jonathan Cape: London.
Fischer, A. H. (1995) 'Emotion concepts as a function of gender', in J. A. Russell, J.-M. Fernández-Dois, A. S. Manstead and J. C. Wellenkemp (eds) *Everyday Conceptions of Emotion: An Introduction to the Psychology, Anthropology and Linguistics of Emotion*. Kluwer Academic Publishers: Dorchrecht, the Netherlands.
Fischer, A. H. (ed.) (2000) *Gender and Emotion: Social Psychological Perspectives*. Cambridge University Press: Cambridge.
Fischer, A. H. and Manstead, A. S. R. (2000) 'The relation between gender and emotion in different cultures', in A. H. Fischer (ed.) *Gender and Emotion: Social Psychological Perspectives*. Cambridge University Press: Cambridge.
Fisher, G. A. and Chon, K. K. (1989) 'Durkheim and the social construction of emotions', *Social Psychology Quarterly*, 52, 1: 1–9.
Flyvbjerg, B. (2001) *Making Social Science Matter: Why Social Inquiry Fails and How it Can Succeed Again*. Cambridge University Press: Cambridge.
Foley, S. (2003) 'Durex in talks to buy sex-aid manufacturer', *The Independent*, 27 October, p. 18.
Foucault, M. (1980) *The History of Sexuality*, Volume One: *An Introduction*. Vintage Books: New York.
Fox, M. F. (1999) 'Gender, hierarchy, and science', in J. S. Chafetz (ed.) *Handbook of the Sociology of Gender*. Kluwer Academic/Plenum Publishers: New York.
Freud, S. (1930) *Civilization and Its Discontents: Complete Psychological Works*, Standard edition, Volume 21. Hogarth: London.
Freund, P. E. S. (1998) 'Social performances and their discontents: the biopsychosocial aspects of dramaturgical stress', in G. Bendelow and S. J. Williams (eds) *Emotions in Social Life: Critical Themes and Contemporary Issues*. Routledge: London and New York.
Frodi, A., Macaulay, J. and Thome, P. R. (1977) 'Are women always less aggressive than men? A review of the experimental literature', *Psychological Bulletin*, 84, 4: 634–660.

Fromm, E. (1974) *The Anatomy of Human Destructiveness*, Jonathan Cape: London.

Furedi, F. (2004) *Therapy Culture: Cultivating Vulnerability in an Uncertain Age*. Routledge: London and New York.

Gallagher, N. W. (1993) 'The gender gap in popular attitudes toward the use of force', in R. H. Howes and M. R. Stevenson (eds) *Women and the Use of Military Force*. Lynne Rienner Publishers: Boulder and London.

Gergen, M. (2001) 'Social constructionist theory', *Encyclopedia of Women and Gender*, Volume Two. Academic Press: San Diego, CA.

Giddens, A. (1992) *The Transformation of Intimacy: Sexuality, Love and Eroticism in Modern Societies*. Polity Press: Cambridge.

Gilligan, C. (1982) *In a Different Voice: Psychological Theory and Women's Development*. Harvard University Press: Cambridge, MA and London.

Glover, J. (2001) *Humanity: A Moral History of the Twentieth Century*. Pimlico: London.

Goldstein, J. H. (1989) 'Beliefs about human aggression', in J. Groebel and R. A. Hinde (eds) *Aggression and War: Their Biological and Social Bases*. Cambridge University Press: Cambridge.

Goldstein, J. S. (2001) *War and Gender: How Gender Shapes the War System and Vice Versa*. Cambridge Unviversity Press: Cambridge.

Goleman, D. (1995) *Emotional Intelligence: Why It Can Matter More than IQ*. Bloomsbury: London.

Gorna, R. (1992) 'Delightful visions: from anti-porn to eroticizing safer sex', in L. Segal and M. McIntosh (eds) *Sex Exposed: Sexuality and the Pornography Debate*. Virago Press: London.

Grant, J. (1993) *Fundamental Feminism: Contesting the Core Concepts of Feminist Theory*. Routledge: New York and London.

Grant, L. (1991) 'Why men want to do it their way', *New Statesman and Society*, 1 November, pp. 30–31.

Gray, J. (1992) *Men are From Mars, Women are From Venus: A Practical Guide for Improving Communication and Getting What You Want in Your Relationships*. HarperCollins: New York.

Greenwald, R. (2004) *Fifteen Steps to Finding a Husband After Thirty*. Time-Warner: London.

Griffiths, P. E. (1997) *What Emotions Really are: The Problem of Psychological Categories*. The University of Chicago Press: Chicago.

Groebel, J. and Hinde, R. A. (eds) (1989) 'Editorial', *Aggression and War: Their Biological and Social Bases*. Cambridge University Press: Cambridge.

Guillaumin, C. (1995) *Racism, Sexism, Power and Ideology*. Routledge: London.

Hacking, I. (1995) *Rewriting the Soul: Multiple Personality and the Sciences of Memory*. Princeton University Press: Princeton, NJ.

Hacking, I. (1999) *The Social Construction of What?* Harvard University Press: Cambridge, MA.

Hall, S. (2002) 'Mother accused of killing babies', *The Guardian*, 20 February, p. 5.

Haraway, Donna, J. (1990) *Primate Visions: Gender, Race, and Nature in the World of Modern Science*. Routledge: London.

Haraway, Donna J. (1991) *Simians, Cyborgs and Women: The Reinvention of Nature*. Free Association Books: London.

Haraway, Donna J. (1997) *Modest Witness @ Second Millennium FemaleMan Meets Onco Mouse: Feminism and Technoscience*. Routledge: London.

Harding, Sandra (1986) *The Science Question in Feminism*. Open University Press: Buckingham.

Harding, Sandra (1991) *Whose Science? Whose Knowledge? Thinking from Women's Experience*. Open University Press: Buckingham.

Harlow, H. F. (1974) *Learning to Love*. Jason Aronson: New York.

Harré, R. (ed.) (1986) *The Social Construction of Emotions*. Basil Blackwell: Oxford.

Harré, R. and Parrott, W. G. (1996) *The Emotions: Social, Cultural and Biological Dimensions*. Sage: London.

Harris, I. M. (1995) *Messages Men Hear: Constructing Masculinities*. Taylor & Francis: London.

Harrison, D. (2003) 'Violence in the military community', in P. R. Higate (ed.) *Military Masculinities: Identity and the State*. Praeger: Westport, Connecticut and London.

Harvey, P. and Gow, P. (1994) *Sex and Violence: Issues in Representation and Experience*. Routledge: London.

Hatfield, E. and Rapson, R. L. (1993) *Love, Sex and Intimacy: Their Psychology, Biology, and History*. HarperCollins College Publishers: New York.

Hatfield, E. and Sprecher, S. (1986) 'Measuring passionate love in intimate relations', *Journal of Adolescence*, 9: 383–410.

Hausman, B. L. (1995) *Changing Sex: Transsexualism, Technology, and the Idea of Gender*. Duke University Press: Durham, NC, and London.

Heidenshohn, F. (1996) *Women and Crime*, 2nd edition. MacMillan Press Ltd: London.

Helgeson, V. S. (1995) 'Masculinity, men's roles, and coronary heart disease', in D. Sabo and D. F. Gordon (eds) *Men's Health and Illness: Gender, Power and the Body*. Sage: Thousand Oaks.

Hendrick, S. S. and Hendrick, C. (1992) *Romantic Love*. Sage: Newbury Park.

Herdt, G. (ed.) (1994) *Third Sex, Third Gender: Beyond Sexual Dimorphism in Culture and History*. Zone Books: New York.

Hill, A. (2002) 'Women to get sex toys on the NHS', *The Observer*, 29 September.

Hill, A. (2003) 'Women log on for one-night stands', *The Observer*, 19 October, p. 7.

Hinsliff, G. (2002a) 'New dads get raw deal from bosses', *The Observer*, 20 October, p. 1.

Hinsliff, G. (2002b) 'Cherie wants fewer women locked up', *The Observer*, 29 September, p. 16.

Hochschild, A. R. (1983) *The Managed Heart: The Commercialization of Human Feeling*. University of California Press: Berkeley, CA.

Hochschild, A. R. (2003) *The Commercialization of Intimate Life: Notes from Home and Work*. University of California Press: Berkeley, CA.

Hockey, J. (2003) 'No more heroes: masculinity in the infantry', in P. R. Higate (ed.) *Military Masculinities: Identity and the State*. Praeger: Westport, Connecticut and London.

Hollway, W. (1984) 'Gender difference and the production of subjectivity', in J. Henriques, W. Hollway, C. Urwin, C. Venn and V. Walkerdine (eds) *Changing the Subject: Psychology, Social Regulation and Subjectivity*. Methuen: London and New York.

Howes, R. H. and Herzenberg, C. L. (1993) 'Women in weapons development: the Manhatten Project', in R. H. Howes and M. R. Stevenson (eds) *Women and the Use of Military Force*. Lynne Rienner Publishers: Boulder and London.

Huntingford, F. A. (1989) 'Animals fight, but do not make war', in J. Groebel and R. A. Hinde (eds) *Aggression and War: Their Biological and Social Bases*. Cambridge University Press: Cambridge.

Hyde, J. S. and Mezulis, A. H. (2001) 'Gender difference research: issues and critique', *Encyclopedia of Women and Gender: Sex Similarities and Differences and the Impact of Society on Gender*, Volume One. Academic Press: San Diego, CA.

Illouz, E. (1997) *Consuming the Romantic Utopia: Love and the Cultural Contradictions of Capitalism*. University of California Press: Berkeley, CA.

Jackson, S. and Scott, S. (2002) 'Introduction: the gendering of sociology', in S. Jackson and S. Scott (eds) *Gender: A Sociological Reader*. Routledge: London and New York.

Jacobs, P. A., Brunton, M. and Melville, M. M. (1965) 'Aggressive behaviour, mental subnormality and the XYY Male', *Nature*, 208, 5017: 1351–1352.

Jagger, E. (2001) 'Marketing Molly and Melville: dating in a postmodern, consumer society', *Sociology*, 35, 1: 39–57.

James, N. (1989) 'Emotional labour: skill and work in the social regulation of feeling', *The Sociological Review*, 37, 1: 15–42.

James, W. (1901; orig. 1890) *The Principles of Psychology*, Volumes 1 and 2. Macmillan: London.

Jamieson, L. (1998) *Intimacy: Personal Relationships in Modern Societies*. Polity Press: Cambridge.

Johnson, S. and Meinhof, U. H. (ed.) (1997) *Language and Masculinity*. Blackwell: Cambridge, MA.

Josephson, W. L. and Colwill, N. L. (1978) 'Males, females and aggression', in H. M. Lips and N. L. Colwill (eds) *The Psychology of Sex Differences: Research Perspectives and Problems*. Prentice-Hall: Englewood Cliffs, NJ.

Katz, J. (1995) *The Invention of Heterosexuality*. Penguin: New York.

Keller, E. F. (1992) *Secrets of Life, Secrets of Death: Essays on Language, Gender and Science*. Routledge: New York and London.

Kennedy, H. (1992) *Eve was Framed: Women and British Justice*. Chatto & Windus: London.

Kessler, S. J. and McKenna, W. (1985) *Gender: An Ethnomethodological Approach*. The University of Chicago Press: Chicago.

Kindlon, D. and Thompson, M. (1999) *Raising Cain: Protecting the Emotional Life of Boys*. Michael Joseph: London.

King, Y. (1989) 'The ecology of feminism', in J. Plant (ed.) *Healing the Wounds: The Promise of Ecofeminism*. Green Print: London.

Klein, U. (2003) 'The military and masculinities in Israeli Society', in P. R. Higate (ed.) *Military Masculinities: Identity and the State*. Praeger: Westport, Connecticut and London.

168   *References*

Langford, W. (1999) *Revolutions of the Heart: Gender, Power and the Delusions of Love*. Routledge: London and New York.

Laqueur, T. (1990) *Making Sex: Body and Gender from the Greeks to Freud*. Harvard University Press: Cambridge, MA.

Larner, J. (2003) 'Why dads are happy to hold the baby' (Jobs and Money), *The Guardian*, 1 November, p. 12.

LaRossa, R. (1997) *The Modernization of Fatherhood: A Social and Political History*. The University of Chicago Press: Chicago and London.

Lewis, G. (2002) *Mobilising Gender Issues*. Report from the Living for Tomorrow Project on Youth, Gender and HIV/AIDS Prevention. NIKK: Oslo.

Lightdale, J. R. and Prentice, D. A. (1994) 'Rethinking sex differences in aggression: aggressive behaviour in the absence of social roles', *Personality and Social Psychology Bulletin*, 20, 1: 34–44.

Lissey, F. J., Klodin, V. and Matsuyama, S. S. (1973) 'Human aggression and the extra Y chromosome: fact or fantasy?', *American Psychologist*, 28: 674–682.

Lloyd, G. (1984) *The Man of Reason: 'Male' and 'Female' in Western Philosophy*. Methuen: London.

Lombroso, C. (1911) *Crime: Its Causes and Remedies*, Patterson Smith: Montclaire, NJ.

Lorenz, K. (1966; orig. 1963) *On Aggression*. Harcourt Brace Jovanovich: New York.

Luhmann, N. (1998) *Love as Passion: The Codification of Intimacy*. Stanford University Press: Stanford, CA.

Lutz, C. (1996a) 'Cultural politics by other means: gender and politics in some American psychologies of emotions', in C. F. Graumann and K. J. Gergen (eds) *Historical Dimensions of Psychological Discourse*. Cambridge University Press: Cambridge.

Lutz, C. (1996b) 'Engendered emotion: gender, power, and the rhetoric of emotional control in American discourse', in R. Harré and W. Gerrod Parrott (eds) *The Emotions: Social, Cultural and Biological Dimensions*. Sage: London.

Maccoby, E. E. and Jacklin, C. N. (1974) *The Psychology of Sex Differences*. Stanford University Press: Stanford, CA.

Madden, T. E., Barrett, L. F. and Pietromonaco, P. R. (2000) 'Sex differences in anxiety and depression: empirical evidence and methodological questions', in A. H. Fischer (ed.) *Gender and Emotion: Social Psychological Perspectives*. Cambridge University Press: Cambridge.

Manderson, L. and Jolly, M. (eds) (1997) *Sites of Desire, Economies of Pleasure: Sexualities in Asia and the Pacific*. The University of Chicago Press: Chicago and London.

Manstead, A. S. R. (1998) 'Gender differences in emotion', in B. McVicker Clinchy and J. K. Norem (eds) *The Gender and Psychology Reader*. New York University Press: New York and London.

Marquit, D. G. and Marquit, E. (1991) 'Gender differentiation, genetic determinism, and the struggle for peace', in A. E. Hunter (ed.) *On Peace, War, and Gender: A Challenge to Biological Explanations*. The Feminist Press: New York.

Marriott, E. and Mondino, J.-B. (2003) 'Men and porn', *The Guardian Weekend*, 8 November, pp. 45–47, 89.

Marsiglio, W. (ed.) (1995) *Fatherhood: Contemporary Theory, Research and Social Policy*. Sage: Thousand Oaks.

Matthews, J. (2003) *Women and War*. Pluto Press: London.

McDougall, W. (1926; orig. 1908) *An Introduction to Social Psychology*. Methuen: London.

McElhinny, B. (1994) 'An economy of affect: objectivity, masculinity and the gendering of police work', in A. Cornwall and N. Lindisfarne (eds) *Dislocating Masculinity: Comparative Ethnographies*. Routledge: London and New York.

McIntosh, M. (1992) 'Liberalism and the contradictions of sexual politics', in L. Segal and M. McIntosh (eds) *Sex Exposed: Sexuality and the Pornography Debate*. Virago Press: London.

McKie, R. (2002) 'Nasal spray for women who are sniffy about sex', *The Observer*, 29 September, p. 1.

Meek, J. (2003a) 'Speaking a different language: but we've got the phrasealator', *The Guardian*, 31 March, p. 1.

Meek, J. (2003b) 'This is not the face of a peacekeeper. I'm doin' the Last of the Mohicans kinda thing', *The Guardian*, 8 April, p. 3.

Miller, M. M. and Riechert, B. P. (2000) 'Interest group strategies and journalistic norms: news media framing of environmental issues', in S. Allan, B. Adam and C. Carter (eds) *Environmental Risks and the Media*. Routledge: London and New York.

Ministry of Defence (2002) Women in the Armed Forces. Summary Report (May) http://www/mod.uk/linked-files/women-af-summary.pdf.

Miringoff, M.-L. (1991) *The Social Costs of Genetic Welfare*. Rutgers University Press: New Brunswick, NJ.

Moir, A. and Jessel, D. (1991) *BrainSex: The Real Difference Between Men and Women*. Mandarin: London.

Moir, A. and Moir, B. (1998) *Why Men Don't Iron: The Real Science of Gender Studies*. Harper Collins: London.

Moore, L. J. and Clarke, A. E. (1995) 'Clitoral conventions and transgressions: graphic representations in anatomy texts, C1900–1991', *Feminist Studies*, 21, 2: 255–301.

Moore, L. J. and Clarke, A. E. (2001) 'A traffic in cyberanatomies: sex/gender/ sexualities in local and global formations', *Body and Society*, 7, 1: 57–96.

Morgan, D. (1994) 'Theatre of war: combat, the military, and masculinities', in H. Brod and M. Kaufman (eds) *Theorizing Masculinities*. Sage: Thousand Oaks.

Morris, B. (1994) *Anthropology of the Self: The Individual in Cultural Perspective*. Pluto Press: London.

Morsbach, H. and Tyler, W. J. (1986) 'A Japanese emotion: *Amae*', in R. Harré (ed.) *The Social Construction of Emotions*. Basil Blackwell: Oxford.

Mullan, J. (2004) 'Let your fingers do the talking', Review, *The Guardian*, 14 February, p. 13.

Murdock, G., Petts, J. and Horlick-Jones, T. (2003) 'After amplification: rethinking the role of the media in risk communication', in N. Pidgeon,

R. E. Kasperson and P. Slovic (eds) *The Social Amplification of Risk*. Cambridge University Press: Cambridge.

Muroi, H. and Sasaki, N. (1997) 'Tourism and prostitution in Japan', in M. Thea Sinclair (ed.) *Gender, Work and Tourism*. Routledge: London and New York.

Naffine, N. (1987) *Female Crime: The Construction of Women in Criminology*. Allen & Unwin: North Sydney.

Naffine, N. (ed.) (1995) *Gender, Crime and Feminism*. Dartmouth: Aldershot.

Nelkin, D. (2000) 'Less selfish than sacred? Genes and religious impulse in evolutionary psychology', in H. Rose and S. Rose (eds) *Alas, Poor Darwin: Arguments Against Evolutionary Psychology*. Jonathan Cape: London.

Norton-Taylor, R. (2002) 'Women still barred from frontline military duties', *The Guardian*, 23 May, p. 6.

Orr, A. (2004) *Meeting, Mating, and Cheating: Sex, Love and the New World of Online Dating*. Reuters: Upper Saddle River, NJ.

Oudshoorn, N. (1994) *Beyond the Natural Body: An Archeology of Sex Hormones*. Routledge: London and New York.

Overing, J. and Passes, A. (eds) (2000) *The Anthropology of Love and Anger: The Aesthetics of Conviviality in Native Amazonia*. Routledge: London and New York.

Oyama, S. (1991) 'Essentialism, women, and war: protesting too much, protesting too little', in A. E. Hunter (ed.) *On Peace, War, and Gender: A Challenge to Biological Explanations*. The Feminist Press: New York.

Oyewùmí, O. (1997) *The Invention of Women: Making an African Sense of Western Gender Discourses*. University of Minnesota Press: Minneapolis.

Payne, K. E. (2001) *Different but Equal: Communication Between the Sexes*. Praeger: Westport, Connecticut and London.

Pease, A. and Pease, B. (2001) *Why Men Don't Listen and Women Can't Read Maps*. Orion Books Ltd: London.

Petersen, A. (1998) *Unmasking the Masculine: 'Men' and 'Identity' in a Sceptical Age*. Sage: London.

Petersen, A. (1999) 'The portrayal of research into genetic-based differences of sex and sexual orientation: a study of "popular" science journals, 1980 to 1997', *Journal of Communication Inquiry*, 23, 2: 163–182.

Petersen, A. (2001) 'Biofantasies: genetics and medicine in the print news media', *Social Science and Medicine*, 52, 8: 1255–1268.

Petersen, A. (2004) 'Research on men and masculinities: some implications of recent theory for future work', *Men and Masculinities*, 6, 1: 54–69.

Pleck, J. (1981) *The Myth of Masculinity*. The MIT Press: Cambridge, MA.

Raafat, N. (2003) 'Lessons in love' (Life Health), *OM*, 2 November, p. 77.

Reddy, W. M. (2001) *The Navigation of Feeling: A Framework for the History of Emotions*. Cambridge University Press: Cambridge.

Rheinberger, H.-J. (1995) 'Beyond nature and culture: a note on medicine in the age of molecular biology', *Science in Context*, 8, 1: 249–263.

Ribot, T. H. (1911) *The Psychology of Emotions*, 2nd edition. The Walter Scott Publishing Co., Ltd: New York and Melbourne.

Richardson, D. (ed.) (1996) *Theorising Heterosexuality: Telling it Straight*. Open University Press: Buckingham.

Roberts, Y. (2003) 'Are you tough enough?', *The Observer*, 11 May, p. 17.

Rochlin, G. (1973) *Man's Aggression: The Defence of the Self*. Constable: London.

Rochlin, G. (1980) *The Masculine Dilemma: A Psychology of Masculinity*. Little, Brown and Co.: Boston.

Rodgers, J. (2003) 'Icons and Invisibility: gender, myth, 9/11', in D. K. Thussu and D. Freedman (eds) *War and the Media*. Sage: London.

Rose, H. and Rose, S. (eds) (2000) *Alas, Poor Darwin: Arguments Against Evolutionary Psychology*. Jonathan Cape: London.

Rose, N. (1989) *Governing the Soul: The Shaping of the Private Self*. Routledge: London and New York.

Rose, N. (1996) 'Power and subjectivity: critical history and psychology', in C. G. Grauman and K. J. Gergen (eds) *Historical Dimensions of Psychological Discourse*. Cambridge University Press: Cambridge.

Rose, N. (1999) *Powers of Freedom: Reframing Political Thought*. Cambridge University Press: Cambridge.

Rosoff, B. (1991) 'Genes, hormones and war', in A. E. Hunter (ed.) *On Peace, War, and Gender: A Challenge to Biological Explanations*. The Feminist Press: New York.

Rotundo, A. (1993) *American Manhood: Transformations in Masculinity from the Revolution to the Modern Era*. Basic Books: New York.

Rowley, H. and Grosz, E. (1990) 'Psychoanalysis and feminism', in S. Gunew (ed.) *Feminist Knowledge: Critique and Construct*. Routledge: London.

Russett, C. E. (1989) Sexual *Science: The Victorian Construction of Womanhood*. Harvard University Press: Cambridge, MA.

Rutherford, J. (1992) *Men's Silences: Predicaments in Masculinity*. Routledge: London.

Sappol, M. (2002) *A Traffic of Dead Bodies: Anatomy and Embodied Identity in Nineteenth Century America*. Princeton University Press: Princeton.

Schiebinger, L. (1986) 'Skeletons in the closet: the first illustrations of the female skeleton in eighteenth-century anatomy', *Representations*, 14 (Spring): 42–82.

Schiebinger, L. (1989) *The Mind Has No Sex? Women in the Origins of Modern Science*. Harvard University Press: Cambridge, MA.

Schiebinger, L. (1990) 'The anatomy of difference: race and sex in eighteenth century science', *Eighteenth Century Studies*, 23, 4: 387–405.

Scott, J. P. (1958) *Aggression*. The University of Chicago Press: Chicago.

Segal, L. (1990) *Slow Motion: Changing Masculinities, Changing Men*. Virago Press: London.

Segal, L. (1992) 'Sweet sorrows, painful pleasures: pornography and the perils of heterosexual desire', in L. Segal and M. McIntosh (eds) *Sex Exposed: Sexuality and the Pornography Debate*. Virago Press: London.

Segal, L. and McIntosh, M. (eds) (1992) *Sex Exposed: Sexuality and the Pornography Debate*. Virago Press: London.

Segal, M. W. (1982) 'The argument for female combatants', in N. L. Goldman (ed.) *Female Soldiers: Combatants or NonCombatants?* Greenwood Press: Westport, Connecticut.

Segal, M. W. (1995) 'Women's military roles cross-nationally: past, present, and future', *Gender & Society*, 9, 6: 757–775.

172   *References*

Seidler, V. J. (1989) *Rediscovering Masculinity: Reason, Language and Sexuality*. Routledge: London.
Seidler, V. J. (1997) *Man Enough: Embodying Masculinities*. Sage: London.
Seitz, B., Labao, L. and Treadway, E. (1993) 'No going back: women's participation in the Nicaraguan Revolution and in Postrevolutionary movements', in R. H. Howes and M. R. Stevenson (eds) *Women and the Use of Military Force*. Lynne Rienner Publishers: Boulder and London.
Shields, S. (2000) 'Thinking about gender, thinking about theory: gender and emotional experience', in A. H. Fischer (ed.) *Gender and Emotion: Social Psychological Perspectives*. Cambridge University Press: Cambridge.
Shields, S. A. (2002) *Speaking from the Heart: Gender and the Social Meaning of Emotion*. Cambridge University Press: Cambridge.
Shilling, C. (1993) *The Body and Social Theory*. Sage: London.
Solomon, R. C. (1993) *The Passions: Emotions and Meaning of Life*. Hackett Publishing Company: Indianapolis.
Spain, D. (1992) *Gendered Spaces*. The University of North Carolina Press: Chapel Hill and London.
Spender, D. (1980) *Man Made Language*. Routledge & Kegan Paul: London, Boston, Melbourne and Henley.
Stearns, P. N. (1993) 'Girls, boys, and emotions: redefinitions and historical change', *The Journal of American History*, 80, 1: 36–74.
Stein, A. and Plummer, K. (1996) '"I can't even think straight": "queer" theory and the missing sexual revolution in sociology', in S. Seidman (ed.) *Queer Theory/Sociology*. Blackwell: Cambridge.
Steinberg, D. (1997) *Bodies in Glass: Genetics, Eugenics, Embryo Ethics*. Manchester University Press: Manchester and New York.
Stephenson, C. M. (1982) 'Feminism, pacifism, nationalism, and the United Nations decade for women', *Women's Studies International Forum*, 5, 3/4: 287–315.
Sternberg, R. J. (1986) *Construct Validation of a Triangular Theory of Love*. Unpublished Manuscript. Yale University: New Haven.
Sternberg, R. J. (1999) *Cupid's Arrow: The Course of Love through Time*. Cambridge University Press: Cambridge.
Stockard, J. (1999) 'Gender socialization', in J. Saltzman Chafetz (ed.) *Handbook of the Sociology of Gender*. Kluwer Academic/Plenum Publishers: New York, Boston, Dordrecht, London, Moscow.
Summerskill, B. (2001) 'Women voice war fears', *The Observor*, 23 September, p. 5.
Tavris, C. (1998) 'The science and politics of gender research: the meanings of difference', in D. Bernstein (ed.) *Gender and Motivation*. Volume 45 of the Nebraska Symposium on Motivation. University of Nebraska Press: Lincoln.
Theweleit, K. (1987) *Male Fantasies*, Volume One: *Women, Floods, Bodies, History*. University of Minnesota Press: Minneapolis.
Theweleit, K. (1989) *Male Fantasies*, Volume Two: *Male Bodies: Psychoanalyzing the White Terror*. Polity Press: Cambridge.
Thomson, M. (2002) 'Boys will be boys: addressing the social construction of gender', in F. Cleaver (ed.) *Masculinities Matter! Men, Gender and Development*. Zed Books: London.

Thorndike, E. L. (1921; orig. 1913) *Educational Psychology*, Volume 1: *The Original Nature of Man*. Teachers College, Columbia University: New York.

Thornhill, R. and Palmer, C. T. (2000) *A Natural History of Rape: Biological Bases of Sexual Coercion*. The MIT Press: Cambridge, MA and London.

Thussu, D. K. and Freedman, D. (2003) 'Introduction', in D. K. Thussu and D. Freedman (eds) *War and the Media*. Sage: London.

Tiefer, L. (1998) 'Challenging sexual naturalism: the shibboleth of sex research and popular sexology', in D. Bernstein (ed.) *Gender and Motivation*. Volume 45 of the Nebraska Symposium on Motivation. University of Nebraska Press: Lincoln.

Tiger, L. (1969) *Men in Groups*. Vintage: New York.

Tooby, J. and Cosmides, L. (1992) 'The psychological foundations of culture', in J. H. Barkow, L. Cosmides and J. Tooby (eds) *The Adapted Mind: Evolutionary Psychology and the Generation of Culture*. Oxford University Press: New York.

Tooley, J. (2002) *The Miseducation of Women*. Continuum: London and New York.

Tumber, E. and Prentoulis, M. (2003) 'Journalists under fire: subcultures, objectivity and emotional literacy', in D. K. Thussu and D. Freedman (eds) *War and the Media*. Sage: London.

Tuten, J. M. (1982) 'The argument against female combatants', in N. L. Goldman (ed.) *Female Soldiers: Combatants or NonCombatants?* Greenwood Press: Westport, Connecticut.

Tyler, D. (1997) 'At risk of maladjustment: the problem of child mental health', in A. Petersen and R. Bunton (eds) *Foucault, Health and Medicine*. Routledge: London.

Van Den Wijngaard, M. (1991) 'The acceptance of scientific theories and images of masculinity and femininity: 1959- 1985', *Journal of the History of Biology*, 24, 1: 19–49.

Venn, C. (1984) 'The subject of psychology', in J. Henriques, W. Hollway, C. Urwin, C. Venn and V. Walkderdine (eds), *Changing the Subject: Psychology, Social Regulation and Subjectivity*. Methuen: London and New York.

Vines, G. (1993) *Raging Hormones: Do They Rule Our Lives?* Virago Press: London.

Vulliamy, E. (2003) 'The killing of film star Marie Trintignant at the hands of her rock star lover has split France in two: some say it was brutal murder, others a crime of passion', *The Observer Magazine*, 16 November, 28–39.

Wajcman, J. (1999) *Managing Like a Man: Women and Men in Corporate Management*. Allen & Unwin: St Leonards.

Walby, S. and Olsen, W. (2002) *The Impact of Women's Position on the Labour Market on Pay and Implications for UK Productivity*. Report to Women and Equality Unit, November 2002. Women and Equality Unit, Department of Trade and Industry: London.

Walkerdine, V., Lucey, H. and Melody, J. (2001) *Growing Up Girl: Psychosocial Explorations of Gender and Class*. Palgrave: Houndmills.

Ward, L. and Smithers, R. (2002) 'Fall of the cabinet golden girl who refused to play the political game', *The Guardian*, 24 October, p. 3.

Warren, K. J. (ed.) (1994) *Ecological Feminism*. Routledge: London and New York.

Washburn, P. (1993) 'Women and the peace movement', in R. H. Howes and M. R. Stevenson (eds) *Women and the Use of Military Force*. Lynne Rienner Publishers: Boulder and London.

Watney, S. (1997) *Policing Desire: Pornography, AIDS and the Media*. 3rd edition. Cassell: London.

Watson, E. A. and Mears, J. (1999) *Women, Work and Care of the Elderly*. Ashgate: Aldershot.

Weare, K. and Gray, G. (2003) *What Works in Developing Children's Emotional and Social Competence*. Research Report No. 456. The Health Education Unit, Research and Graduate School of Education, University of Southampton.

West, C. and Zimmerman, D. H. (1991) 'Doing gender', in J. Lorber and S. A. Farrell (eds) *The Social Construction of Gender*. Sage: Newbury Park, CA.

Western, D. (1999) *Mind, Brain and Culture*, 2nd edition. John Wiley & Sons: New York.

Whittaker, D. J. (2001) 'Definition of terrorism', in D. J. Whittaker (ed.) *The Terrorism Reader*. Routledge: London and New York.

Wierzbicka, A. (1999) *Emotions Across Languages and Cultures*. Cambridge University Press: Cambridge.

Wiggings, J. S., Renner, K., Clore, G. L. and Rose, R. J. (1971) *The Psychology of Personality*, Free Press: Boston, New England.

Wilson, E. (1992) 'Feminist fundamentalism: the shifting politics of sex and censorship', in L. Segal and M. McIntosh (eds) *Sex Exposed: Sexuality and the Pornography Debate*. Virago Press: London.

Wilson, E. O. (1975) *Sociobiology: The New Synthesis*. The Belknap Press of Harvard University Press: Cambridge, MA and London.

Wintour, P. and Watt, N. (2002) 'Morris quits: "I've not done as well as I should have" ', *The Guardian*, 24 October, p. 1.

Witkin, H. A., Mednick, S. A., Schulsinger, F., Bakkestrom, E., Christiansen, K. O., Goodenough, D. R., Hirschhorn, K., Lundsteen, C., Owen, D. R., Philip, J., Rubin, D. B. and Stocking, M. (1976) 'Criminality in XYY and XXY men', *Science*, 193, 4253: 547–555.

Women and Equality Unit (2004) *Gender Briefing, January 2004*. Department of Trade and Industry: London.

Woodward, R. and Winter, P. (2003) Gendered bodies, personnel policies and the culture of the British Army (January). Final report for ESRC.

Worell, J. (ed.) (2001) *Encyclopedia of Women and Gender: Sex Similarities and Differences and the Impact of Society on Gender*, Volume 1. Academic Press: San Diego, CA.

Wouters, C. (1991) 'On status competition and emotion management', *Journal of Social History*, 24, 4: 699–717.

Wouters, C. (1998) 'Changes in the "lust balance" of sex and love since the sexual revolution', in G. Bendelow and S. J. Williams (ed.) *Emotions in Social Life: Critical Themes and Contemporary Issues*. Routledge: London and New York.

Yalom, M. (2001) *A History of the Wife*. Pandora: London.

Yanagisako, S. and Delaney, C. (eds) (1995) *Naturalizing Power: Essays in Feminist Cultural Analysis*. Routledge: New York and London.

Young, E. (1996) 'Confederate counterfeit: the case of the cross-dressed civil war soldier', in E. K. Ginsburg (ed.) *Passing and the Fictions of Identity*. Duke Univeristy Press: Durham and London.

Young, I. M. (1990) *Justice and the Politics of Difference*. Princeton University Press: Princeton, NJ.

Younge, G. (2003) 'US state to allow gay marriage', *The Guardian*, 19 November, p. 2.

Yul-Davis, N. (1997) *Gender and Nation*. Sage: London.

Zillman, D. (1984) *Connections Between Sex and Aggression*. Lawrence Erlbaum Associates: NJ.

Index

emotion – *continued*
  psychological studies of, 53
  social constructionist
    approach to, 4
  war, gender and, 57–64
  women, the military and, 69–79
emotional, being, 5
  see also feminine, being
emotional deficits, 128, 137, 144
emotional dumping, 134
emotional explosions, 129–30
emotional expression standards, 6–7
Emotional Intelligence, 128,
emotional intelligence, 129, 130–1
emotional intimacy, 115, 121
emotional labour, 4, 5, 8, 27,
    138–42, 144–5
  'work on the self', 8
emotional liberty, 7, 8
Emotional Life of Nations, The, 60
emotional literacy, 27, 124, 125–44
  politics of, 128–34
Emotional Literacy Handbook, The,
    133
emotional management, 4, 7, 127,
    130, 136, 138, 142, 143–4
  'failure of boys', 136–7
  styles, 7
emotional navigation, 7, 8
emotional regime, 7, 8
  according to Reddy, 7
  strict, 7–8
emotional self, 4
  -mastery, 130
emotional work, 4, 94, 107
emotionality with irrationality,
    association of, 5
emotions
  as irrational, 5
  central to life of individuals, 7
  cultural patterns of, 52–3
  cultural view of, 6
  engendering, 2–5
  expressing, 86
  notion of control (Lutz's view), 6
  people talking about, 5–6
  political significance of, 7–8

psychology of, 3, 10
social constructionist approach to,
    52–3
in sociology, 24–5
subject to social influence, 7
engendered emotions, concept of,
    2–7
English, D., 16
Enloe, C. H., 70, 74
equal opportunities policies, 23
equality feminism, 22
equality versus 'celebration of
    difference', 21–5
Erickson, J. A. (with Steffen, S. A.),
    116
essential difference, 28
Evans, M., 92, 122, 157
'evil axis', 15
evolutionary psychology
  definition of, 36–7
  focus of species-specific
    adaptations, 37
  framework of, 37–8

face-painting, 68
'falling in love', 26, 91, 94–5, 101,
    110, 121
Family Circle, 108
Fausto-Stirling, A., 18, 39, 46, 93
feeling rules, 144
female coyness, 35
femaleness *see* femininity
feminine, 22
  being, 5
  see also femininity
feminism
  object-relations theory, 36
  and the field men and masculinity
    studies, 9
  studies of difference stereotyping
    women, 10
  see also femininity
femininity, 35, 120–1
  association of emotion to, 16
  depressed, 16
  pacifism and, 77
  weakness as sign of, 14